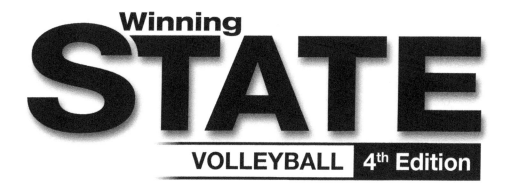

Winning STATE

VOLLEYBALL 4th Edition

The Athlete's Guide To Competing Mentally Tough

Join the select group
of mentally tough athletes
who handle the nerves,
fiercely compete,
and win.

WinningSTATE
The Mental Toughness Company

DEDICATION

To my first genuine coach and mentor, who for years patiently taught me many of the methods and techniques that are presented in the following pages—experiences and skills that provided more than just a solid foundation for my sports career—I dedicate the 4th editions of the *WinningSTATE®* *Mental Toughness Series* to him.

Additionally, to *all* of the coaches who unselfishly and tirelessly help others get ahead in sports and life.

"Steve Knight is one of the few American Powerlifters who displays the mental control and confidence of the European Olympic Lifters."
Bill Starr, Author
Defying Gravity: How To Win At Weightlifting
The Strongest Shall Survive: Strength Training for Football

Front Cover: Lauren Cook.
             Photo by *HMFRphotos/www.flickr.com/hmfrphotos*
Back Cover: Candace Lee.
             Photograph by *Jamie Schwaberow/NCAA Photos*

Library of Congress Catalog Control Number: 2005905528
Publisher's Cataloging-in-Publication (By Let's Win! International).

 Let's Win! ® International, Portland, OR 97201
Mental Toughness Training 4.0

WinningSTATE ® 4–Volleyball: The Athlete's Guide To Competing Mentally Tough / by Steve Knight—4th ed.
            p. cm.
ISBN: 979-8-9882909-5-7
1. Sports 2. Psychology 3. Volleyball
1. Knight, Steve ll. Title. 9 8 7 6 5 4 3 2

Printed in the United States of America

ACKNOWLEDGEMENTS

Many people contributed to *WinningSTATE—VOLLEYBALL* and I am happy to acknowledge their help and thank them here.

Indirectly, Steve Krug, "Don't Make Me Think," gave us the muddle and test frame we use for more than just our website; Scott McCloud, "Understanding Comics," provided us with the fundamentals for sequential art storytelling; and Phil Knight, who during an interview jokingly commented that Coach Bowerman was a "professor of competitive response," which gave us "primal competitive reaction," the floor under the *WinningSTATE* Mental Toughness System.

Then there are the artists who brought our concepts to life: Jason Cheeseman-Meyer, the best penciler around; Chris Horn, inker extraordinaire; and Dan Jackson, a fabulous painter.

Now, to those in the kitchen with their hands in the soup: to Martin and Lilly at Copyman Press, who consistently provide us top-quality printing; to Leah Sims who gives us absolutely pristine text; to Bo Johnson of Bowler Hat Comics, who helped us think of storytelling in a visual way; and Layne Ross, who pushed through seventy key language drafts and hours of banter to help shape our delivery; and to Ryan Peinhardt, who assisted with a new layout and graphics, and to Travis Torgerson, who did the fine tuning of the 4th edition text flow and chapter ends. Thanks to everyone!

To Peter McKittrick, whose "gut" reactions and direct challenge, at pivotal points, changed our direction and the "technology;" to Casey Cox, whose contribution to "the system" was significant; and to Nick Bahr, whose production contribution is so broad and deep it's in a category by itself. Thanks to you all!

And to Nick Gilardi, whose focus on the "flow and the content of each chapter" in the 4th edition better presented each skill, and additionally had a defining impact on the system in general. Thank you!

Finally, I am deeply grateful to those who patiently guide and mentor me as I bumble through life's steady stream of decisions.

PREFACE

In 1974, at 19 years old, I entered my first weightlifting tournament. I barely knew the lifts, and knew even less about *the process* of a tournament. I was totally in the dark about competing. My only previous sports experience had been Little League baseball.

I placed last, but was bitten by the competition bug. I loved the challenge of delivering under pressure in a "theater" setting. I quickly figured out that performing on demand was entirely mental and that "confidence" was not the missing ingredient to handling the nerves. A different skillset was needed that had nothing to do with set and reps, hard physical work, or how I "felt" about myself. The missing ingredients were mental toughness and focus, both of which require a tournament process and specific focus points to concentrate on.

I went on to spend eleven years as a competitive weightlifter, winning several state and two national championships, and was ranked 2nd in the world. I lifted in the 181 lb weight class, and in 1982 set an Oregon state record in the Squat of 722 lbs that still stands today.

Due to the scarcity of how-to resources on the mental side of competing I often wondered how a book providing world-class mental toughness skills would be received. In the fall of 2001 I began writing *WinningSTATE-Wrestling* with the intention of equipping wrestlers with an organized process to bring order to chaotic tournament environments, and with specific focus points to handle the nerves, believe in themselves, compete, and win.

WinningSTATE-Wrestling was so well received, and the demand from other sports was so high, over the past 11 years we expanded the series to 16 titles that include paper books, audio books, (mobile apps), and an online mental toughness academy. The *WinningSTATE* Mental Toughness System has become the world leader in mental toughness training for athletes who need to win—*WinningSTATE* athletes.

Now let's learn how to compete, mentally tough.

WinningSTATE-VOLLEYBALL

TABLE OF CONTENTS

INTRODUCTION: EVERYONE GETS NERVOUS

WinningSTATE
The Mental Toughness Company

INTRODUCTION
EVERYONE GETS NERVOUS

Everyone gets nervous performing in public. Everyone! The goal is to use the nervous energy to our advantage. The goal is to build a mental game that withstands the intensity of the public spotlight. Achieving this goal puts us in that select group of mentally tough athletes who think their way through the nerves and get it done—*WinningSTATE* athletes.

Consider this: sports experts have said for decades that "Competing is 90% mental" or some version of "Competing is all in your head." Those aren't slogans. Competitive sports are about winning, and winning under pressure requires a second set of skills: mental toughness skills.

Buckle up. The following will (1) dispel two myths that are holding you back, (2) provide a simple overview of how your two brains operate under pressure, and (3) inspire you to build a mentally tough mental game.

Physical Sweat Is Not Enough

In the fifteenth century the general belief was that the sun revolved around the earth. Eventually, science proved that the earth revolves around the sun. In the sports world today there's a general belief that physical sweat is what produces mental toughness when it's showtime and that hard physical work is what we draw on to handle nerve-racking pressure. We disagree. We argue that physical sweat has very little to do with handling nerves.

To explain: Performance athletes on all levels, including professionals, who are physically skilled, strong, and conditioned, hesitate in high-pressure situations—repeatedly. That would not be the case if physical sweat were the answer to handling nerves. We believe mental toughness skills are

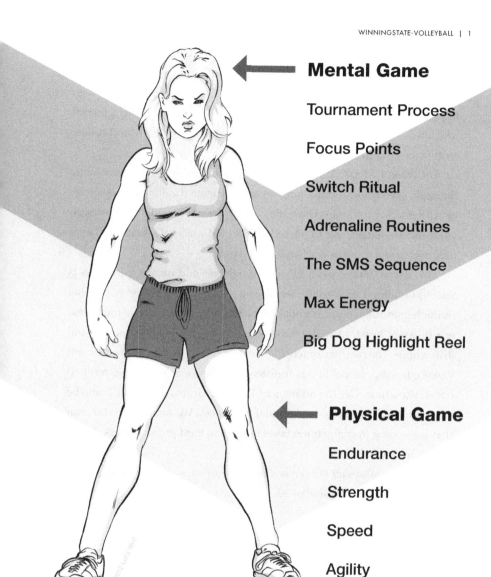

Mental Game

Tournament Process

Focus Points

Switch Ritual

Adrenaline Routines

The SMS Sequence

Max Energy

Big Dog Highlight Reel

Physical Game

Endurance

Strength

Speed

Agility

WinningSTATE ATHLETES

WinningSTATE athletes bring both of their games together on match day to compete mentally and physically tough and get the win.

what we use to boldly step into the competitive spotlight and, say, "Watch this," and then actually do it. That perform-on-demand attitude that generates the "I can do this under the lights" self-belief isn't achieved through improved strength, speed, and conditioning. It's achieved through mental toughness. Mental toughness is what's needed to think clearly and competently when our heart is pounding and our mind is racing.

The *WinningSTATE* Athletes illustration on page 1 drives the point home. Strength, speed, and conditioning do not eliminate dwelling on negativity or surrendering to doubt. Have they yet? They never will. Hard physical work increases believing in oneself a little, but physical sweat will never produce mental toughness when it's showtime.

This distinction between physical toughness and mental toughness is vital to building a rock-solid mental game. Physical toughness is pushing through pain and fatigue; it's not being a physical wimp. Mental toughness is a different beast; mental toughness is strictly dealing with nerves and distractions. The two, like practice and competition, are drastically different. Practice is safe, competition is threatening. Practice is learn-time, competition is showtime. Get the difference? We must draw a thick black line between physical toughness and mental toughness. We must be crystal clear that succeeding in competition takes more than hard physical work. It also takes hard mental work.

• *Point: we must shift our perspective to relying on mental toughness skills to handle the nerves, not physical sweat.*

Some Have It, Some Don't

Along with rejecting the "physical sweat is enough" belief, we also reject the thinking that some of us have "it," and some of us don't.

This belief (trait theory) suggests that our ability to handle the nerves is determined by our parents, who either pass along the handle-the-nerves gene or they don't. Please. To suggest that we're either born with mental toughness or we're not is missing the obvious: Even world-class veterans, those who supposedly have "it," struggle with self-belief. In a millisecond we all shift from believing to doubting, then back to believing, and then back to doubting, emotionally flip-flopping around like fish out of water. Doubt in general is a constant issue for human beings, but especially for competitive athletes. Our self-belief is on public display, and it changes from moment to moment and year to year. Genetic traits are consistent; our eyes don't change color due to mood swings. Handling the nerves is not determined by our genes. Handling nerves is an active, adaptable attitude acquired through life experiences and mental toughness skills, not static genetic traits.

We believe overcoming our "apprehensive" reactions, the primal first tendency for most of us, is the challenge. Most of us react negatively to any task that includes the potential of failure. Instead of focusing on what might go right, we dwell on what might go wrong. Most of us give in to thoughts and feelings of possible failure and embarrassment without any fight, and it's 100% in our heads. Handling nerves is not a genetic gift that only a few have been blessed with. Handling nerves comes down to training our concentration and choosing what to focus on.

Handling nerves comes down to training our concentration and choosing what to focus on.

• *Point: all of us have the genes to handle the nerves; the task is to build a mentally tough mental game so we can focus.*

Realize that you have "it." Attack mental toughness skill-building with the same passion you have for the physical side of sports. Commit! Become a mental game giant.

The next section is handling pressure 101. Every performance athlete must know basic brain science.

Basic Brain Science

There's a small part of our brain responsible for our reactions to threatening situations, such as performing in public. It's called the amygdala (a-mig-da-la), which we simply refer to as nerves. And when our nerves flare, one of our two primary brains takes over, either our levelheaded left brain or our emotional right brain.

Basic brain science dictates that pressure creates fear, fear creates adrenaline, adrenaline creates nerves, and nerves create confusion. Don't get trapped in the thinking that at some point you'll be nerve-free—that's a

© 2012 Let's Win!

OUR LEFT BRAIN

Our left brain's response to nerves
is levelheaded, mentally tough
and doubt free.

fallacy. To be mentally tough under the lights, we must first stop avoiding nerves.

Look over Our Left Brain vs. Our Right Brain illustrations above. Read the captions. Our believer left brain vs. our doubter right brain. We're either in control or out of control. We're either dominated by self-belief or we're consumed with negative nonsense. That's the real battle! Right? And as performance athletes it's a never-ending battle.

OUR RIGHT BRAIN

Our right brain's reaction to nerves is apprehensive, mentally weak and hesitant.

The broad goal of mental toughness skill-building is to loosen the grip of our doubter right brain by increasing the dominance of our believer left brain. Levelheaded thinking is how we stay mentally tough and focused on the battlefield. In other words, if we can't think levelheaded and control our emotions, we can forget about consistently performing well at a high level. The metaphoric Ice Man is 100% levelheaded.

• *Point: the Doubt Demons don't stand a chance when we make our levelheaded left brain the dominant voice in our head.*

Note: Neuroscience (brain science) is advancing at a fast pace. Many experts assert that the right/left theory is oversimplified and that the brain is much more complicated. That may eventually prove to be true. Our intention is not to promote the right/left theory but rather to utilize a common understanding that our left hemisphere is where logic takes place (map reading, math calculations, engineering, structure, etc.), while our right hemisphere is emotional, random, creative, and imaginative.

As competitors wanting to deliver our best, we don't have the luxury of uncontrolled emotional outbursts. They are our undoing.

Whether the brain functions exclusively right or left, or a combination of both hemispheres, no one can deny that our brain has two voices, levelheaded and emotional. The question for us to consider is this: When our nerves flare, which one of our brains has the loudest voice?

Now it's time to introduce our real opponents: the 3 Doubt Demons.

The 3 Doubt Demons

Nerves are NOT the enemy. The 3 Doubt Demons are the enemy. As competitors wanting to deliver flawless execution under the lights, we must know exactly what gets under our skin. We must face the 3 Doubt Demons head-on, because they're relentless. Dealing with our apprehensive, doubtful, pessimistic, hesitant reactions is a constant battle. As we discussed, even athletes at the highest levels, professionals and Olympians, are never free of apprehension or negative thinking.

• *Point: don't think "someday" you'll be so cool that apprehension under pressure won't be an issue—we always second-guess ourselves and always will.*

Here's why: The Demon of Inadequacy presents mental images of our weaknesses, the Demon of Past Failure reminds us of not-so-great past performances, and the Demon of Embarrassment projects thoughts and feelings of potential humiliation. Weird, isn't it? Why are we so self-defeating?

Why do we smother ourselves in apprehension and doubt rather than pump ourselves up with real-world "facts" that inspire our self-belief.

Strange as it sounds, apprehension is a hardwired part of our self-preservation response, which helps us avoid danger and seek safety. However, competitive environments are anything but safe, so we must be able to override those primal apprehensive reactions. As competitors we have chosen high risk and social danger, so we must toughen-up, *switch attitudes*, and boldly face the nerves and the public scrutiny.

Our real opponents, the 3 Doubt Demons, are most active when we're minutes or seconds away from a clutch opportunity. Our nerves explode and we channel that amazing adrenaline straight into self-doubt. Then, the Doubt Demons talk us out of what we can do and into what we can't do.

That's why we must acquire the mental weapons to come to our own defense. The Doubt Demons are intently waiting for the slightest crack in our self-belief. We must be armed, vigilant, and ready to crush their nonsense. We'll talk more about the 3 Doubt Demons in the coming chapters, but for now realize that no one is free of apprehension and doubt under pressure, not even Navy SEAL recruits.

Navy SEAL Water Competency

Whoa! Navy SEAL training—talk about needing to switch attitudes to overcome fear and intimidation. Navy SEAL methods for doing this are similar to *WinningSTATE* mental toughness skill-building (even though we didn't get our skills from them and they didn't get theirs from us).

Check this out: To become a Navy SEAL one must pass several competencies. The third competency, water competency, is the best example of utilizing mental toughness skills to stay levelheaded and not freak out under extreme threat. The primary SEAL concern is that if we can't *think* during life-or-death situations, we jeopardize both ourselves and our team. The water competency ordeal quickly brings to the surface (literally) those who get overwhelmed by the extreme super-fear of drowning.

Picture a huge pool about fifteen feet deep with a surface area at least the size of a basketball court. The sides of the pool are far away when you're out in the middle. A recruit is equipped with a scuba mask, flippers, and a mouthpiece connected by hoses to an air apparatus on his back. In the water along with the recruit are several SEAL instructors with bad intentions.

To pass water competency, a recruit must stay submerged for twenty minutes, never surfacing, while SEAL instructors mess with him from all angles: right, left, behind, above, and below. One instructor is pulling on his mask while another is messing with his air hose. Just as the recruit gets his equipment back in place and is ready to take a breath—BAM!—

WinningSTATE athletes focus their mental weapons on crushing doubt rather than trying to inflate their "confidence."

another attack from a different angle. The intent of the relentless attacks is to simulate the feeling of drowning, which determines a recruit's freak-out response. Can he stay composed and think his way through the intense super-fears or does he come emotionally unglued and need to surface? If a recruit surfaces before the twenty minutes are up, he fails. Recruits get four attempts at passing the dreaded water competency. And 77% fail all four attempts. Failing means exiting SEAL training. Talk about pressure.

After failing the first attempt, recruits are sent to mental toughness classes to learn how to talk themselves through the primal super-fear reaction. The recruits who pass water competency with their new mental toughness skills demonstrate the ability to keep from panicking under extreme threat, or to panic, recover, and fight back, and in doing so take one more step toward becoming Navy SEALs.

Important note: SEAL recruits are not sent to learn how to "physically work harder class" or "inspiration class," they're sent to "learn how to confront their primal super-fears head-on class." Now I'm not doggin' the physical side of sports or emotional inspiration. I'm putting them in perspective. Of course we must train hard physically, and of course pound-your-chest emotion is uplifting, but under pressure it's levelheaded, objective thinking we use to get the job done.

• *Point: confronting our apprehensive reactions head-on is critical to doubt-free execution under the lights.*

Note: go to winninstate.com and watch the Discovery Channel's Navy SEAL video—very impressive to say the least.

A *WinningSTATE* Advantage

Gaining a *WinningSTATE* advantage produces the ability to conquer the biggest problem in sports: the nerves.

An organized tournament process. Specific focus points. A ritual to switch attitudes. Max energy. The SMS Sequence. Adrenaline Routines. Responsiveness to apprehension. The ability to draw on past success. *WinningSTATE* athletes bring these mental toughness skills and routines to the battlefield—a definite competitive advantage.

Gaining a *WinningSTATE* advantage starts with the perspective that (1) winning is mental and we must shift our perspective from physical sweat to mental sweat, and (2) confidence is overrated. Doubt is the enemy. When we don't doubt, we're "confident." *WinningSTATE* athletes focus their mental weapons on crushing doubt rather than trying to inflate their "confidence."

Along with shifting perspective, gaining a *WinningSTATE* advantage requires building mental toughness vocabulary. Words are a necessity. To do "it" we must be able to think about "it," and to think about "it" we must be able to talk about "it," which requires vocabulary. Don't underestimate the power of words.

Caution: Most of us are intimidated by new information, because new information is confrontational—it either makes us feel uninformed or it messes with our established viewpoint. To put it bluntly, most of us are new-information pansies. We cling to what we know instead of pursuing what we don't know. *WinningSTATE* athletes don't automatically shut out new information; they take it in and evaluate its value.

• *Point: we must build mental toughness vocabulary to match the vocabulary we have for the physical side of sports to add a new dimension to our game.*

After perspective and vocabulary, gaining a *WinningSTATE* advantage is accomplished by constructing a tournament process that includes easily engageable focus points. This is how we eliminate distractions and crush apprehension. Think about it. Practices are highly organized and very specific, but we go to tournaments (the reason we practice) without a clue of "what to do." Our mental game is built around an organized process and specific focus points that anchor our self-belief when our nerves feel like the sparking loose end of an electric cable.

Along with shifting perspective, expanding vocabulary, and constructing a tournament process with specific focus points, we must become skilled at using The Big 3: self-talk, visualize, and adapt. No matter how scary of a dragon we're facing, we must be able to (1) engage in levelheaded self-talk, (2) strictly visualize positive images, and (3) constantly adapt. All of the *WinningSTATE* mental toughness skills and routines are accessed through The Big 3: self-talk, visualize, and adapt.

Take a breath. Don't expect to breeze right through this. It's new! Just put in some effort and in no time you'll possess an entirely new approach to competition: a mental toughness approach.

• *Point: be a mental game giant.*

Which brings us to: you already have "it."

You Already Have "It"

Grasp the fact that you already have "it." You don't need to travel to a foreign land in search of mental toughness. You already have what it takes to respond to pressure with a level head. Just realize that pulling off clutch performances by believing in yourself is an active, personal choice, not a random event. We must train ourselves in the art of choosing to believe rather than allowing ourselves to doubt—it's up to us!

Let's do a quick recap: physical sweat is not enough, all of us have the genes to handing the nerves, basic brain science dictates that the nerves are unavoidable, and the 3 Doubt Demons are the real enemy.

Adapt! Add your most powerful weapon to your competitive arsenal: *your mind.* Build a tournament process with specific focus points to stay levelheaded and doubt-free when the expectations are huge and all eyes are on you.

Are you convinced? The previous information should have sold you on the fact that solid performances are in every one of us if we believe it. So believe! Work your mental game to command a winning state of mind. Join the select group of mentally tough athletes who think their way through the nerves, compete, and win—*WinningSTATE* athletes.

THE GOAL

Mental Toughness Under Pressure

The goal is to see performing in public through a new set of eyes.

The goal is to build a mentally tough mental game that skillfully handles the nerves and nails the execution.

The goal is to be a mental game giant.

Compete mentally tough!

WinningSTATE
The Mental Toughness Company

1 SWITCH
GET FIERCE

What lights your fire? Is your competitive backbone spaghetti or tempered steel? Do you stand your ground, *switch attitudes* and fight back, or do you blink, hesitate, and surrender? Guaranteed, we all have a tremendous amount of fierce, fight-back power. We just need to unleash it.

F ight back! Become skilled at *switching* from friendly to confrontational. If we can't deliberately SWITCH from our friendly attitude to our confrontational attitude with conviction, we're toast. Competition demands it! *WinningSTATE* athletes leave Ms. Congeniality in the parking lot.

Nerves of steel require switching attitudes, and switching attitudes must be as easy as flipping a light switch. The question is not whether we have a fierce, confrontational Big Dog attitude to switch to but whether we can unleash it and have the skills to control it.

To switch attitudes we must know our two dogs.

Our Little Dog vs. Our Big Dog

All of us—there are no exceptions—have Little Dog *reactions* and Big Dog *responses* to the challenges of performing in public. To gain control of our nerves and let our fierceness out, we must know our two dogs.

Our Little Dog is fearful and apprehensive. Our Little Dog gets overwhelmed by nerves, distractions, and formidable opponents. Under pressure, our Little Dog fears the spotlight, can't think, comes emotionally unglued, and melts down.

"Unleash your fierce, fight-back, confrontational attitude. Let your Big Dog out!"

Our Big Dog is fearless and brave. Our Big Dog faces the nerves head-on, easily switches from friendly to confrontational, and loves a good battle. Under pressure, our Big Dog welcomes the spotlight, keeps a level head, draws on success, and boldly executes.

Which of our two brains is the source of our Big Dog fierceness? Yep, our levelheaded left brain. Our apprehensive right brain is the source of our Little Dog. Our fierce Big Dog is not interested in emotional nonsense. Our fierce Big Dog is only concerned with one thing: doubt-free execution.

• *Point: we all have a fierce Big Dog attitude just waiting to come out.*

For example: Check out this grandma story. Not my grandmother, but a grandmother. We've all heard the story of the woman who lifted a car off her son to save his life. But since we didn't witness it, we question it. Well, this grandma story took place in Colorado, early 2007, and was documented on the evening news.

A stereotypical grandma and grandpa in their seventies are hiking in bear country—grizzly bear country. Unfortunately, the elderly couple crosses paths with a grizzly who decides Grandpa is going to be lunch. The bear attacks and has Grandpa by the throat—literally tasting blood— but Grandma decides no way, bear, not today. Screaming over and over, "Fight back, don't give up!" to her husband while ferociously thrashing the bear with a big stick, Grandma drives the bear off and saves their lives.

Cut to the hospital room. Grandpa's head, neck, shoulders and one arm are in bandages. He looks like a wounded soldier just returned from the battlefield. When asked what happened, Grandpa can only mutter, "She saved our lives; I gave up." Frail, gray-haired Grandma can't even relate to what she has done, and fiddling with a tissue in a weak, high voice whispers, "Well, sometimes we do what we must," while humbly looking to the floor.

Whatever, Gram, you're a stud!

-3 Terrified   -2 Panicked   -1 Tweaked

THE GRR METER

The Grr Meter displays our emotional reactions to nerves. Too much aggression is just as disastrous as too much apprehension. How does pressure affect you?

The point is, Grandma and Grandpa's bear encounter confirms we are all born with a Big Dog attitude deep inside, the power to assert our will, to fight back against adversity of all kinds, to overcome threats, pain, intimidation, and hardship—the list is long.

The problem is that in social situations, our fierce Big Dog can quickly escalate from being assertive to being overly aggressive. And like highly unstable plutonium, our Big Dog is often associated with being out of control. So we avoid and repress it, rather than learn how to command and use it. But to be a mentally tough, successful competitor, we must be able to unleash our Big Dog and control our Grr Factor, which translates into a winning, fight-back attitude

Our Grr Factor

In nervy, go-time situations we all have an extreme range of emotional reactions, from terrified to fuming, which the Grr Meter illustrates on pages 14 and 15. Our Grr Factor is our will, our fight-back power, and too much Grr (the fuming end of the Grr Meter) is just as detrimental as too little Grr (the terrified end). Neither is levelheaded.

+1 Fierce   +2 Angry   +3 Fuming

Superwoman juice (adrenaline) is not our Grr Factor. Adrenaline is automatic. It's predictable and reliable—adrenaline is our friend. Our Grr Factor is what we do with the Superwoman juice. Our Grr Factor is our "attitude." If our apprehensive Little Dog reactions are in control, we channel the adrenaline straight into self-doubt. But if our fierce Big Dog responses are in control, we channel the adrenaline straight into self-belief and conviction.

• *Point: our Grr Factor, our will, controls the Superwoman juice (or not).*

So the double task is to (1) climb into our fierce Big Dog attitude, and (2) control the adrenaline. We must think about our competitive emotions (our nerves) in order to handle them. That requires mental toughness vocabulary, specific mental pictures, and adapting. It's important to get our mind around those three ideas. Can you describe your two brains, your two dogs, and your Grr Factor?

Note: This is the "work" part of building a mental game. Being mentally active and considering new ways of thinking requires mental sweat. And adapting is never easy. However, if we want to improve and succeed, we

"If you really want to succeed in this competitive world, you have to love a challenge."
Mike Reid

SWITCH to your attacker or protector Big Dog attitude!

must evaluate and adapt. Which brings us to a decision you need to make: Are you an attacker or a protector?

Switch: Attacker or Protector?

For some of us, switching to assertive and confrontational while maintaining control of our passion is a no-brainer. But for others our aggressive, passionate side can be uncomfortable and difficult to deal with. However, all performance athletes must take on a fiercely focused competitive attitude. That's how we fight back, compete, and win.

Are you an attacker or a protector? This attacker-protector analogy helps us visualize our Big Dog's "nature." But, whether we're attackers or protectors, both attitudes are assertive and confrontational.

Assertive? Confrontational? Absolutely! No question. Most performance athletes don't think like that. Competition turns us inside out, laying us bare. And for many of us, our competitive backbone is more spaghetti than tempered steel. The only way to change that is to get some attitude—a doubt-free attitude with some swagger. Ask yourself: Are you an attacker or a protector?

The obstacle to achieving this confrontational attitude is overcoming our social conditioning—how we were taught to behave. Most of us are conditioned from birth to be modest, kindhearted, gentle, and compassionate, and definitely not to show off. Those socially conditioned attitudes are the absolute opposite of what is needed to succeed in competition. It's just the way it is.

Look at the *Switch* illustration on page 19. Engage the radically different attitudes. They're black-and-white—oil and water. Notice the expression differences. Can you feel the attitudes behind those faces? Compare the captions. Which guy would you want on your team? Ask yourself: Do you identify with bold, assertive, and selfish? Or do you identify more with modest, agreeable, and giving?

For many of us this deep attitude change from friendly to confrontational is a monstrous challenge. For example: Ms. Congeniality types who are friendly, kind, and giving must radically alter their attitudes to either attackers or protectors to succeed in competition. Why? Friendly, kind, and giving get crushed in competition. Competing is aggressive, territorial, and very revealing. In other words, there's only one trophy and one rule: it must be taken! Permission is not required, nor will it ever be given.

Mentally tough competitors who get it done think (1) "It's mine. Get out of my way. I'm taking this," (2) "Not today, there's no way you're taking this from me," or a combination of both. That attacker or protector mentality is at the core of every successful competitor.

There's only one trophy and one rule: it must be taken! Permission is not required, nor will it ever be given.

Period. End of story. When two competitors have this bring-it-on mentality and can back it up with core mental toughness and excellent physical skills, then we have a heated, nose-to-nose, winner-take-all competition.

• *Point: before stepping onto the court, switch to a Big Dog attacker or protector attitude, so you can compete and win, not just participate.*

Here's an additional example of a fight-back attitude that may help you decide, if you haven't already, whether you're an attacker or a protector: Which dog are you in the following scene?

Picture a dog chewing on a bone while another dog approaches and attempts to take the bone. I don't think so. The dog with the bone will protect its treasure with all its might. However, the dog trying to take the bone will attack with all its might. Who gets the bone? The dog with the fiercer Big Dog attitude, of course.

In competition we must deliberately separate our friendly "let's get along" social attitude from our confrontational "I'm going to knock your head off" competitive attitude. Competition requires switching and letting our fierce Big Dog out. Think about it. Practice is psychologically challenging, of course, but competition is extreme.

What lights your fire? What's inside of you? What's your competitive backbone made of? Will you stand your ground and fight back? Or do you blink, hesitate, and surrender? We all have more fight-back power than we realize, we just need to unleash it. *WinningSTATE* athletes don't allow their mind to be dominated by social conditioning or doubt. *WinningSTATE* athletes let their Big Dogs out—for real, no pretending, and no holding back!

To succeed under pressure we must have a go-to process, a ritual to switch to the part of us that will bravely step up, face the heat, and boldly compete. Guess what. Coach can't switch for us, we must do it ourselves.

Another way to get our mind around switching from friendly to competitive is picturing fierceness. "You could see the *fierceness* in their eyes," describes mentally tough *WinningSTATE* athletes.

Fierceness

For many of us switching to a fierce attitude means being angry, the fuming end of the Grr Meter. But it's not. Fierceness is an intensely determined, deliberate mindset—a levelheaded, focused mindset that turns the Superwoman juice into an advantage—a single-minded attitude that's only concerned with fighting back and winning.

• *Point: a fierce, deliberate, doubt-free attitude is what separates those who get it done from those who don't.*

Many athletes have learned how to look fierce. They have the right body language and facial expressions, but their insides are still spaghetti, not steel. Making faces and trying to look focused and fierce are not a part of a deep-down, get-it-done attitude. They're just posturing. Posturing is childish and full of hot air—it's an act, not an attitude.

Weightlifters can be the worst at posturing—yelling, slapping, huffing and puffing. Do they think they're intimidating the weights? I don't think so. Or some might say, "That's what gets me up." Again, I don't think so. In most cases it's an outward display of fear. They're scared to death and fall victim to nervous "I might fail" reality. They're trying to intimidate their own doubt, which is both a tremendous energy drain and rookie behavior.

Our fierce Big Dog is not social posturing—our fierceness is not an act. Our fierce Big Dog doesn't care who is watching or what they're thinking. Our fierce Big Dog is only concerned with *executing* and *getting it done*.

Fierceness comes from attitude, not anger. No acting, no pretending, no faking, just steely-eyed, armor-piercing concentration. We block out every-

EVERYDAY	COMPETITION
Friendly	Confrontational
Modest	Bold
Agreeable	Assertive
Giving	Selfish

 **SWITCH**

Switch attitudes. Leave Ms. Congeniality in the parking lot. Unleash your bold, confrontational, assertive, fight-back attitude. Fiercely compete to win.

thing except the objective, being completely focused in the present, not lost in emotional, future-obsessing self-doubt. Fierceness comes from an attacker or protector *attitude*.

Here's what fierceness is not: it's not saying to ourselves, "I want it, I want it, I want it," or "I can, I can, I can." That's right-brain emotional garbage. Of course we want it and of course we can. Fierceness doesn't come from chanting positive statements or imagining victory.

Here's what fierceness is: a growling dog. Not an angry, barking dog, a growling dog. Those quiet, low-level, serious growls are the kinds I'm referring to. Like when a female with pups is lying with her head resting on a paw and as we get to the edge of her comfort zone, she gives us that

Fierceness is an intensely determined, deliberate mindset... that turns the Superwoman juice to our advantage...

low-level growl without moving that says, "Hey! One more step and we've got a problem." We stop right there. Why? The mother dog isn't messing around, we know she means business. It's not an act or a game. One more step and she's up baring teeth—some fierce, no-nonsense Grr.

Can you growl? I mean seriously growl. I'm not talking growl and giggle. I'm referring to that deep growl that comes from our gut. When our jaw tightens and our brow wrinkles and our eyes focus intently on a specific target. Yes, our Big Dog attitude is intense and all of you pacifists need to get a grip. Competing is primal, and bloodcurdling fierceness is required or we get run over.

• *Point: don't project your Big Dog, be your Big Dog.*

Are you feeling it? Stuffing tuff competitors, smoking big kill shots, and fighting for great digs are all about fierceness, mental toughness, and our Big Dog Grr Factor. Mentally tough competitors, *Winning-STATE* athletes, realize that a fiercely determined mindset is an absolute necessity to delivering clutch performances, and *switching* from friendly to confrontational is mandatory.

As we finish this chapter, make the connection between our two brains, our two dogs, and our Grr Factor. Answer the question: Are you

Nebraska's Brooke Delano (right) goes for a kill against Texas in the NCAA college volleyball regional finals match inOmaha, Nebraska. Photo by *Nati Harnik/AP Photo*

an attacker or a protector? Buy into the fact that wholehearted, fierce execution is a necessity for *grabbing the prize* or the competition will grab it from us. We must become skilled at *switching attitudes* from socially friendly to competitively confrontational.

Evolve

For most competitors, and warriors throughout history, switching to a "take no prisoners" state of mind is a mandatory pre-battle personal ritual. A paint your face, sharpen your weapon, put on your gear, and take it to 'em ritual. What's your pre-battle ritual? We must be able to turn our Big

Dog fierceness on and off, just like a light switch: click => click. And it must be that simple.

In competition, we must deliberately separate our friendly "let's get along" social attitude from the confrontational "I'm going to knock your head off" competitive attitude. Competition requires switching and letting our fierce Big Dog out.

Get in the moment. Make it crystal clear in your mind you're entering a hostile environment, literally leaving safety behind. Picture the proverbial kill-or-be-killed battleground, where *someone* gets run over and left in the dust. Light the competitive fire in your belly. Adapt. Evolve your fierce, fight-back attitude. That deep-down conviction to fiercely compete that doesn't require showing anybody anything. It's personal—it's totally internal. We're summoning our primal fight-back response to threatening encounters. We're letting our fierce Big Dog out.

• *Point: add a fiercely competitive attitude to your mental game. Switch!*

The following is from The History Channel's description of the DVD series *EVOLVE*:

> *It's a tough, violent, and lethal world out there, and it's been that way since the dawn of time. Roughly 99 percent of all species have become extinct. What enabled that other one percent to survive the cutthroat competition? Their ability to.... EVOLVE.*

Now you know how to *switch* attitudes—and fight back!

GET FIERCE

1 SWITCH

Don't be a pushover. Switch attitudes. Unleash your attacker or protector and fight back.

TOURNAMENT PROCESS

Create your switch ritual. Get serious.

FOCUS POINT

Let your Big Dog out. Don't be angry, be determined.

THE BIG 3

SELF-TALK

"It's you or me. Come on. Bring it on!"

VISUALIZE

Picture dominating with attitude. Step up!

ADAPT

Fierceness wins, friendly doesn't.

WinningSTATE
The Mental Toughness Company

2 NARROW
ELIMINATE DISTRACTIONS

Can you concentrate or are you easily distracted? An unfocused mind gets overwhelmed by tournament chaos. *WinningSTATE* athletes focus on a "tournament process" and specific "focus points" to gain greater control over hostile tournament environments.

Mentally check in! Become skilled at narrowing your focus.

If we can't systematically *NARROW* our focus to just our job and believing in ourselves, poor performances will be the result. *WinningSTATE* athletes forcefully shrink their world down to competing by concentrating on a tournament process and specific focus points that eliminate arena distractions.

Distractions are the enemy, not nerves. Tournament distractions are nonstop. The competition commotion makes for a chaotic, unpredictable experience if we're not mentally equipped. But, just as crushing doubt does not come from our genes, the ability to concentrate and eliminate distractions doesn't either. Blocking out distractions is a simple, repeatable process in which (1) we must be mentally active and (2) we must narrow our concentration to three battle zones, specific focus points, and adrenaline routines. The difficult part is actually doing it on demand.

Mentally active? Three battle zones? Specific focus points? Adrenaline routines? Absolutely! Concentrating is not a white-

"Restrict your focus to SMS and your job at each battle zone."

knuckle situation. When our emotions are churning and the Super-woman juice is pumping through our veins, and numerous distractions are competing for our attention—announcers, fans, coaches, teammates, parents, friends, other matches being played—we must have organized routines and specific focus points to shift our thinking, reduce the chaos, and eliminate distractions.

• *Point: we must have targets to focus on in order to focus.*

Really take in the photo on page 27, the *Battleground*. That's the reason we put in the blood, sweat, and tears—we want to win in competition! We want to succeed in that hostile "all eyes on you" environment that can knock the wind out of many great athletes who would otherwise kick butt at practice.

Distractions are the enemy! If we don't have an organized tournament process that includes specific focus points to concentrate on, we get overwhelmed. That's why again and again we circle back to The Big 3: self-talk, visualize, adapt. Why? Being mentally active and engaging The Big 3 under pressure is how we stay in control and focused, rather than falling victim to distractions and primal fears, and then looking like a deer in the headlights. We focus on factual, inspiring self-talk and visualize realistic mental pictures to deal with the onslaught of stimuli unique to competitive environments. Even if we attempt to duplicate the chaos of a big match in practice, it's not even close to the same intensity level.

• *Point: we eliminate distractions by focusing on go-to mental weapons.*

The 3 Battle Zones technique and the SMS Sequence are those go-to mental weapons. First, we shrink the arena down to 3 Battle Zones to (1) make every arena as familiar as possible to play in and (2) restrict our focus to our job at each battle zone: the stands/

bench, the court, and the service area. Next, we shift our attention to the present Situation, our key Mechanics, and our Big Dog Success (SMS). We use these two *WinningSTATE* techniques to narrow our concentration to what's important: *doubt-free execution.*

Let's break down the SMS Sequence.

The SMS Sequence

As we step into the competitive spotlight, we're either doubting or believing. To 100% believe we must control what gets our attention, because what gets our attention affects what's going on in our head, and what's going on in our head affects the outcome.

Distractions are the enemy! Our minds can only do one thing at a time. We're either focused and on point or we're scattered and off point. We're either concentrating on competing and winning or we're distracted by "the event." If we find ourselves caught up in the tournament commotion, we whack ourselves on the head and click back into the objective—we're there to compete and win, not mess around or get lost in the public scrutiny. We use SMS to narrow our focus down to three main thought categories: the present situation, our key mechanics, and our past success.

Distractions are the enemy! We're either focused and on point or we're scattered and off point.

Here are some examples of SMS in action.

The Present Situation:

"The situation" has broad reach, from daily training expectations to the final points of a big set, and everything in between. Plugging into the situation

THE BATTLEGROUND

The infamous Battleground (right) can be overwhelming. To get comfortable with being under the lights practice visualizing having all eyes staring at you. Then block them out with SMS!

EVERYDAY LIFE　　　　OTHER MATCHES

DISTRACTIONS ARE NONSTOP

Distractions are endless. They come from all directions.
Mentally check in and focus on competing. Block out
distractions by focusing on your job at each battle zone.

means being conscious of what's going on at that moment and what we
should be expecting of ourselves. For example, it's the middle of the day,
our knee is swollen from a hard practice, do we ice immediately and then
once more in the evening or do we blow it off and go hang out? Here's
another example of a situation the morning of a tournament: We woke up
feeling good, ready to compete, and find that family friends came over to
visit and brought donuts and pastries. Do you indulge in the goodies or go
get some Big Dog fuel?

We need to formally organize our physical mechanics, our go-to
skills, so we can easily think about them when distractions are robbing
us of our focus.

Realize that knowing our key mechanics is not being egotistical.
Bragging about our key mechanics is being egotistical. Knowing our
key mechanics is being smart. Having our go-to mechanics in the
front of our mind is our power. Along with our past success, it's what
we can believe in. Our go-to mechanics are what we use to disarm our
opponents. For example, on the bench we narrow our concentration

CRAZY FANS

EVENT CHAOS

down to the situation. "How much time do I have? Am I warm and loose?" Then we visualize our powerful mechanics and polish our solid fundamentals over and over in our head. We gear our self-talk to the game plan and our assignment, "Breathe. Focus. Good release and follow through. I've got this!"

  • *Point: make your primary key mechanics clear in your mind, so you can easily think about them under pressure.*

Now let's move on to our Big Dog success.

Our Big Dog Success:

WinningSTATE athletes view success as pushing through apprehension and overcoming doubt, not winning trophies or putting up points. In other words, when we push through the nervousness and go for it, that's when we win. When we suck-it-up and let our Big Dog out and take a risk, that's success. Sometimes we make the play, sometimes we don't. But when we handle the nerves, free ourselves up, and give it everything we've got, we win, no matter the outcome. Make sense? Pushing through apprehension and overcoming doubtful moments are our Big Dog victories. And we all have thousands of them. We just don't pay attention. We overcome apprehensive reactions in social situations every day. Most of us dwell on negative experiences rather than on "I can't believe I just did that" experiences.

THE "SMS" SEQUENCE

Restrict your mental activity. Concentrate on SMS: the present
situation (S), your key physical mechanics (M), and your past
Big Dog success (S). Repeat the sequence.

We typically require someone else, a parent, coach, or friend to point out
those "Look what you just did" moments. We must learn how to do that for
ourselves. That is the essence of coaching ourselves up.

Appreciate the fact that overcoming apprehension and going for
it goes all the way back to when we were toddlers first starting to
walk. The examples throughout life are endless. Pushing through
our self-preservation reaction can be very difficult. Early in life it
prevents us from physically hurting ourselves, but as we grow and
mature it morphs into embarrassment prevention software. Obviously, much of the time we override nervous apprehension or we'd
never learn to walk or leave the safety of our bedroom.

Chapter 5 lays out a step-by-step process to formally docu-
ment our Big Dog success. For now, realize that we all have a ton
of experiences when we crush apprehension and go for it to draw
on. And those success experiences are what we use to power our
self-belief. For example: "Last year against this team I was scared

MECHANICS

SUCCESS

to death. I was so nervous. I seriously doubted myself, but I told myself it's all in my head and decided to have some fun and we placed 3rd. This year we're going all the way to finals."

• *Point: from this moment on be very aware of your overcoming-doubt experiences, your Big Dog success, both on and off the court.*

Building our SMS focus points is not that difficult, because we already have the necessary vocabulary and specific mental pictures, we just need to organize and prioritize them into three thought categories: the present situation, our key mechanics, and our past Big Dog success. Think, prepare, make connections—be mentally active. This is what building a mental game is all about. Thoughts control the outcome, and organized, systematic thoughts eliminate distractions and enhance our focus on getting it done.

Now let's break down the 3 Battle Zones, the other technique needed to help *narrow* our focus.

The 3 Battle Zones

Yes, indeed, the 3 Battle Zones are physical locations. But the point is not to tell you something you already know. The point is to see all venues in the same way, which helps us better fight the real battle—the one between our ears.

This *WinningSTATE* Battle Zone technique may seem trivial, but it's not. For most of us turning every arena into three mental battle zones that also are the three physical locations where we spend most of our time accomplishes two things: (1) we make every arena as *familiar* and comfortable to play in as possible, and (2) we restrict our focus to our job at each battle zone. This mental process helps eliminate distractions by giving us something to do mentally. We control every tournament (or match) from three battle zone locations: the stands (the bench), the court, and the service area.

• *Point: we make every arena "home" by staking out our territory and knowing our job at each battle zone.*

Let's clarify the *familiarizing* aspect of this 3 Battle Zone technique. All arenas are the same in many ways, so we just need to be mentally active and compare the similarities. If we don't, unfamiliar environments can grow out of proportion and be a major focus breaker. Treat competitive environments as if you're walking across a narrow beam high off the ground. What's the first rule? Don't look down. Why? Because looking down breaks our concentration and engages our fear, causing us to lose our center of balance, stumble, and literally make ourselves fall. Competitive environments present the same kind of concentration challenge. If we aren't prepared for the visual differences, along with the constant barrage of people distractions that are always in our face at some level our focus wanders and we get put off balance. The solution is to turn every arena into three familiar battle zone locations—to stake out our territory and take control of our environment.

• *Point: the stands (the bench), the court, and the service area are similar and very predictable at every arena.*

When we actively familiarize ourselves with all arenas, we reduce the discomfort of a particular arena's layout or size. If we don't, we're playing right into the Doubt Demons' hands. They use arena differences and people distractions to confuse us and attack

THE COURT
Switch. Anticipate. SMS

THE SERVICE AREA
Breathe. Replace. Believe.

THE STANDS/BENCH
Narrow. Fuel. Rest.

© 2012 Let's Win!

⌄⌄ NARROW

The 3 Battle Zones are three familiar locations at every arena. Make every arena "home" by forcefully restricting your activities to your "job" at each battle zone.

our self-belief. And since our mind can only do one thing at a time, we're either mentally weak, getting bombarded by arena distractions, which drains energy, or we're mentally tough, staying strictly focused on our job at each battle zone, which conserves energy.

The other aspect to this technique of seeing all venues as 3 Battle Zones helps us restrict our thinking to our job at each battle zone. In other words, we must know exactly what we need to do at each battle zone to stay focused, composed, and ready to compete.

And most importantly, once we figure out what we should be doing at each location, we must actually do it.

Now let's take a closer look at each of the 3 Battle Zones.

The Stands (The Bench):

At tournaments the stands are where we will spend most of our time, so we'd better figure out how to get comfortable. Picture being at home on the couch chilling out and watching TV. That's the kind of comfortable I'm referring to. Resting before and in between matches is a huge part of physically recovering and mentally adjusting and the stands (the bench for single matches) is where that takes place. Make sure to bring a pillow and sleeping bag with you to multi-match tournaments so you can be comfortable all day. In between matches we need to go back to the stands to fuel, kick in some SMS, and rest till our next warm-up.

> **We must know exactly what we need to do at each battle zone to stay focused and ready to compete.**

In the stands there will be many things trying to prevent you from preparing for your next match. The biggest distractions, other than the Doubt Demons, are friends and family. Yes, friends and family. We all love the support and we know how much that means to us, but as a competitor it's pure distraction. We don't need our mom or boyfriend rubbing our back telling us how wonderful we are. We need to be telling ourselves how awesome we are. We need to fuel, think about what we should be doing at that moment (the situation), focus on SMS, and chill out.

For those of us who can't sit still and calm our minds, music is a great diversion. Put together tournament playlists to easily plug into. For some, reading is very helpful, so we bring along our favorite book or magazine to take our mind off of the competition. Most importantly, we put our head on our pillow, chill out, and rest, rest, rest.

This battle zone is called the stands and not the arena for a reason: we need to be parked in the stands between matches, not running around the arena playing social games. Running around and constantly checking things out is an energy drain and a total distraction. We have a job to do in the stands, so we get over the social thing and do what we should be doing: fueling, hydrating, resting, recovering, and preparing. We sprawl out on our sleeping bag, get comfy, put on some music, and fuel up.

For single matches, there are many mentally positive things to do on the bench besides sip water, catch your breath, and yell. The bench is not only a place to Grr up, but more importantly it's a place to kick in some levelheaded thinking and go over our focus points. We breathe, tell the Doubt Demons to take a hike, and get ready to step out onto the court. If we use our bench time wisely, we'll be mentally ready to participate in those clutch plays during the final points.

The Court:
The court can be a very challenging battle zone. Stepping onto the playing surface can make focusing difficult. Switching is a must at this point. On the court is where the territorial battle begins and the Doubt Demons start whispering in our ear. We try not to get distracted by the event, we focus on ourselves. We stay calm and relaxed. We do this through forceful self-talk. We kick in some SMS, and do our best to keep our nerves as neutral as possible. We are in control, not the event or our primal emotions. Sure, we're amped up and ready to play some volleyball, but mentally and emotionally we stay levelheaded. Of course the nerves spark a little every time we're in the mix, but we give ourselves a drill sergeant like pep talk and refocus on The Big 3.

"The only one who can tell you 'you can't' is you. And you don't have to listen."

Nike

On the court we must deal with endless distractions and numerous doubt triggers. This is why physical routines are so effective. They force our mind to think about the things that put up points, like seeing the whole court, a smooth release, and excellent follow through, rather than thinking about anything else. On the court, we stay mentally alert and conserve energy. We breathe and focus on the positive. We don't want to get caught off guard with even the slightest negativity. We control the internal battle between our doubter right brain and our believer left brain. When our overly emotional right brain is making a lot of noise, we force a self-talk hard-hitting discussion about *why* we can beat who we're matched up against. We talk our way through the nerves in any situation with a level head—our left brain has our back if we'll just engage it.

On the court, we use SMS to narrow our focus to just what's in front of us, our teammates, our opponents, the ball, and the net. We get lots of oxygen and breathe, breathe, breathe. I'm not talking hyperventilating, I'm suggesting loading up on oxygen, and forcefully breathing throughout the match. We coach ourselves up with levelheaded, factual self-talk, push the play button and visualize our Big Dog highlight reel. We convince ourselves we can deliver and go for it. We skillfully believe, not just randomly hope. We step into the play full of self-belief, not apprehension and doubt.

• *Point: be mentally active and crush doubt. Compete mentally tough.*

The Service Area:

As the ref signals it's time, either our Big Dog or our Little Dog steps up to the line. If we're rested and fueled, if we're thoroughly switched on and we're keeping our Grr Factor neutral, if we're staying loose and seriously focusing on SMS, then our Big dog steps up to the line and says "watch this," and nails it. But if we're unprepared and let ourselves get distracted by match-time chaos, our Little Dog steps up to the line mind racing and heart pounding. At that moment, many competitors would rather drop to their knees and make a pact with some kind of universe super force instead of take the heat directly. "Please, just let me make this serve and I'll do anything!" Hoping or repeating positive statements isn't going to get us out of this. We must prepare for the spotlight, because spotlights are intense, confusing, and turn us inside out.

The key to handling the heat is mentally rehearsing for those intense, uncomfortable feelings of being completely alone and being stared at. When we rehearse being the center of attention, that "space" becomes more familiar and less intense, and we can get out of our own way and do what we've trained so hard to do: play tough and compete.

Rehearsing feeling those feelings of being looked at is a huge part of our mental game, because every trip to the line produces the same weird awareness, and always will. We try to focus directly on the situation and the serve, but simultaneously we have a physical sense of all the space around us and everyone who's watching. It's a physical-mental-emotional experience very similar to giving a presentation in front of a group. We acutely see ourselves doing what we're

Visualize being in front of a large crowd. See the faces and feel the stares and all that attention focused on you.

doing, which can be very unnerving. Then, bring the Doubt Demons into the picture and it can be complete mental chaos.

Rehearse. Visualize being in front of a large crowd. See the faces and feel the stares and all that attention focused on you. Then forcefully narrow your focus to just SMS, and confidently say to yourself, "Yeah, everyone's staring at me, so, bring it on!"

Reducing all volleyball arenas to 3 Battle Zones and restricting our focus to SMS helps us bring order to a chaotic environment, rather than allowing our surroundings to confuse and distract us. Practice these two narrowing techniques and there's absolutely no reason to be uncomfortable or distracted at any arena. Every arena is home—mentally we own it.

NARROW your focus to just the SMS Sequence and the three Battle Zones.

Don't Be A Kid At The Park

The discipline required at tournaments, especially travel tournaments, is probably the hardest discipline to master, especially for those who don't travel much. Many non-frequent travelers want to make the most of their travel adventure by running around and constantly socializing.

Here comes the dad/coach, stern-faced, finger-pointing speech: Don't be a kid at the park. Get a grip! Don't lose sight of why you're there. Remember why you've worked so hard and what you want to accomplish. You're there to compete and win! Make positive, disciplined decisions that propel you toward victory, as opposed to leaving you sitting in dejection. Don't be that five-year-old who just got asked if he'd like to go to the park. Can't you see it? Your eyes would get big. You'd be grinning from ear to ear and nodding your head yes, yes, yes. Walking to the park you'd be skipping, jumping, hopping, and bouncing. Once you got sight of the park, off you'd go, and then the screaming, shrieking, yelling, and all-out play would follow. Hate to break it to you, but those days are over. Tournaments are not a park. Settle down and compete.

For many, traveling with their team is a new experience and emotionally they treat it like some sort of vacation. I've seen the distractions at state and nationals derail many would-be champions because they (unconsciously) lost their competitive focus and turned into kids on the monkey bars. They indulged themselves socially because they lacked the perspective and the skills to force themselves to chill out, concentrate, and stay mentally focused on competing. I've seen many great athletes over the years at away tournaments turn into goofy children instead of being steely-eyed, fierce, deliberate competitors.

• *Point: give yourself an advantage when you're off the court by forcing yourself to think like a champion, not like a kid on a playdate.*

I'm not suggesting sitting in the corner of the hotel room in a yoga position with a towel over your head, but if your focus wanders it's likely that come match time you won't be as sharp as you need to be. Tournaments are not a theme park or a backyard barbecue. Don't fall into the trap of mistaking an away match or tournament for some sort of vacation—it's not Disneyland. It's a competition. Yeah, of course we have fun,

Our competitive Big Dog is who needs to be in charge, not our friendly, everyday social self.

but we don't forget why we're there—we're there to compete, and win. We need to stay somewhat reserved most of the time, because we want to store up the Superwoman juice to be as powerful as possible come match time.

One of the key problems with maintaining focus before and during tournaments is dealing with our own pent-up emotions, our teammates' pent-up emotions, our coaches' pent-up emotions, and all our peers' bright, smiling faces. Everyone means well, but mostly it's pure distraction. Our competitive Big Dog is who needs to be in charge, not our friendly, everyday social self. Champions save the messing around for after finals. Then we can go have all the fun we want.

Trust me, tournaments are not the place to play social games. We enjoy our teammates and other athletes from out of town, but our attitude is competitive and our habits are focused, mentally tough, and fiercely determined. We must control what gets our attention. Distractions, both internal and external are the champion destroyers.

Eliminate Distractions

One of the underlying points throughout this chapter, and the entire book, is you already have "it." All of us already have what it takes to eliminate distractions, handle the nerves, *believe*, and win. We don't need to buy new shoes or burn incense to be focused, doubt free, and get it done. We just need an organized tournament process with specific focus points to narrow our concentration and block out distractions. Then we can easily concentrate on what's important: *distraction-free execution.*

WinningSTATE athletes treat all competitive environments as hostile, high-distraction battlegrounds. We mentally check in, switch attitudes, and focus our attention on getting ready for the next match. We use the WinningSTATE narrowing skill to get our mind right. We stay mentally active and give ourselves something to think about. We are in control, not our primal emotions.

Just as we consistently sharpen our offensive and defensive skills to be more consistent and competitive under pressure, we must also build our SMS focus points and be crystal clear about our job at each of the 3 Battle Zones. We must control what gets our attention, because what gets our attention affects what's going on in our head, and what's going on in our head determines whether we make the play or not. Deliberately shrink your world down to competing, so you can nail the execution.

Now you know how to *narrow* your focus—to eliminate distractions.

CHECK IN

2 NARROW

Don't be a kid at the park. Mentally check in and compete. Focus on SMS inside 3 Battle Zones.

TOURNAMENT PROCESS

Set up your battle zones, stakeout your territory.

FOCUS POINT

Concentrate on SMS and your job at the moment.

THE BIG 3

SELF-TALK

"I'm here to compete, not mess around."

VISUALIZE

Picture the SMS Sequence in detail.

ADAPT

Limit your activities to your job.

WinningSTATE
The Mental Toughness Company

3 FUEL
POWER YOUR PERFORMANCE

When you think of food, what comes to mind, taste or energy? Don't be a taste junky! Break free of sugar and convenience. *WinningSTATE* athletes intelligently adapt their food choices to fuel their dream, rather than just lazily pleasing their taste buds. Power your decision-making machine.

Eat to win! Become skilled at *fueling* for competition.

If we can't make *FUEL* choices that power our performance, we run out of gas late in the match. *WinningSTATE* athletes don't focus entirely on taste; they also focus on food choices that provide max energy for quick recovery and on-target decision-making.

Fueling is critical! Other than crushing apprehension and eliminating distractions, I don't know of any other aspect of competing that has greater significance. Bulletproof concentration, excellent decision-making, and crisp execution throughout an entire tournament are what it takes to win. Letting down mentally for one second can alter future opportunities. Why risk a mental error because of an empty gas tank? Don't we want max energy for rock-solid performances? Of course we do. The challenge in this junk-food-heavy environment is seeing food through the winning lens, not just the taste lens.

• *Point: getting our conditioning in is important for quick recovery, but high-octane fueling is just as important.*

"Deliberately fuel to compete. Choose fresh, high-octane carbs and fats over taste."

Update your thinking. Think of food as fuel. Educate yourself. Put in some effort and adapt your food habits. Eliminate sugar!

Food Is Fuel

Check out the *Food Court* illustration on pages 44 and 45. The food imposters on the left page may taste good and are easy to grab 'n go, but those choices offer very little "gas." The examples shown on the right page don't taste bad, they just haven't been flavor enhanced. Those fresh, clean, high-energy food choices are the best power source for quick recovery and crisp decision-making point after point.

Think of food more functionally (what you need) than emotionally (what you want), especially for tournaments. Focus on what your mind and body need to hustle for every dig, block, and kill shot for an entire match (let alone overtime), to quickly recover, and to be ready for the next match, rather than flavor preferences. Make flavor a second priority. Since food is literally competition fuel, choose rocketfuel over poser food.

This isn't that complicated. We don't have to become nutritionists to understand the basic differences between high-octane rocket fuel and no-octane poser food. Stay with me here. Think of food as types and sources. Types: carbs, fats, and proteins. Sources: fresh or processed. Blending carbs and fats from fresh sources is high-octane rocket fuel. Processed junk food is no-octane poser food. It's pretty simple.

Another way to think of food is to link it to building an internal competitive bonfire, one that will roar for hours.

Building A Blazing Bonfire

This "bonfire" metaphor helps us get our mind around the fuel vs. taste conflict. Picture a blazing, open-pit bonfire. See the dancing flames. Smell the smoke. Hear the pops and the crackles. Feel the intense heat from sev-

THE FOOD COURT

The Food Court illustrates the drastic differences between toxic low-energy fuel imposters and fresh high-octane rocketfuel. Choose energy first, flavor second. Eat to win!

eral feet away. Now think of the materials we'd gather to not only build our blazing bonfire, but also to keep it roaring for hours. We'd gather clean paper or dry grass, various sizes of dry twigs, and armfuls of extra dry logs. Now make the connection that fresh carbs and good fats are exactly like the paper, twigs, and dry logs. Simple carbs are the paper or grass, because simple carbs burn quickly and easily. Complex carbs are the twigs,

because complex carbs are denser and burn a little slower. Fats are the dry logs, because fats have twice the energy as carbs. Fats are the coals that our competitive bonfire is built on. Once we get our bonfire going, we throw both types of carbs on top of the coals, and then more logs to keep the coals from dying out. (Low-fat anything should be avoided.) Proteins are like wet, green wood that just lies there smoldering

• *Point: make food choices to fuel your competitive bonfire instead of thinking only about flavor.*

Are you seeing it? Imagine we're on a camping trip with friends and it's time to start a campfire. Are we lazily going to try to start our campfire by lighting green logs with a match? Don't think so. We'd be cold and hungry in no time. Make the connection that fueling for high performance requires choosing the right materials to build an internal competitive bonfire—a roaring bonfire that constantly fuels our decision-making machine and replenishes our physical strength and endurance. Keep this bonfire metaphor in mind throughout this chapter. I explain the best types of paper, twigs, and logs to use at tournaments to get the most out of ourselves when it counts.

Our Decision-Making Machine

Our bodies don't give out first, our minds give out first. Our "will" (our Grr Factor) and our Superwoman juice require actual "gas." Take in the scientific fact that our mind burns real fuel. And it burns a lot of it in competition. If it were possible to get an MRI of our brain just before stepping onto the court, we'd see it light up like a Christmas tree. Our brain would look like a massive emergency response scene with hundreds of emergency vehicles' lights flashing.

Our decision-making machine (our brain) consumes 20% of our total available energy, but what's more important is that our brain cannot store energy—it's completely dependent on a continuous new supply from the bloodstream. In competition our body is performing at peak levels, our mind is on overload consuming 20% of our energy supply, and we expect our physical conditioning to handle the recovery. I don't think so. Think roaring bonfire, not liquid sugar, candy, meat, or other non-energy producing taste items.

• *Point: our decision-making machine needs fresh fuel—frequently!*

Processed junk foods like burgers, fries, shakes, and soda pop, or quickie mart microwave anything are not what our high-performance machine needs to compete at a high level. Our "will," our determination runs on real fuel. Processed junk food is the last thing our mind needs before, during, or after a demanding practice or intense match. Our mind and body need pure energy from two carbs (simple and complex) and good fats. That's what we use to keep our decision-making machine running a peak levels throughout an entire tournament.

University of Nebraska's senior middle hitter Carlie Christensen (left) gets a kill past Wayne State Wildcats blocker #11. Photo by *Staff/www.omavs.com*

Two Carbs & Good Fats

As we touched on previously, carbs are split into two categories: simple (paper) quick carbs, and complex (twigs) slow carbs. As competitors wanting to excel, we need a small amount of simple and a large amount of complex. Most of us get the opposite, a large amount of simple and a small amount of complex. Almost no one gets any fat. But to build and keep our bonfire blazing we need a small amount of paper, a larger amount of twigs, and armfuls of dry logs.

BIG DOG FUEL

Combine paper, twigs, and logs to keep your competitive fire blazing. Choose high-octane carbs and fats from fresh sources. No meat. No sugar!

Think of fruit as simple carbs (like paper). Fruit is the quickest energy to get into the bloodstream. Our bodies instantly burn natural fruit sugar. Note: not all sugars are created equal, which I'll explain in the next section.

Natural whole grains (bread and pasta), brown rice, and some fresh vegetables are the complex carbs (like twigs). Our bodies have to work a little harder at burning complex carbs, but they provide a longer-burning, more stable energy stream, unlike fruit (paper), which is—*poof*—gone.

Fats are the least understood, but the most important *fuel* for our roaring bonfire. Our bodies love fat because it's concentrated, dense energy. There is twice as much caloric energy in one gram of fat than there is in one gram of carbohydrate. Fats are the dry logs for our body's competitive bonfire.

Some of the misinformation you may have read or heard includes the idea that fat slows digestion. That's incorrect. The right way to look at fat

Paper
Fast-Burning Carbs

Twigs
Slow-Burning Carbs

Logs
Long-Burning Fats

is that it's *slower to digest*. Since fat has twice the energy as carbs, it burns slower, which is a good thing.

Example: Think of trying to keep a bonfire blazing for hours. If we just use paper and twigs, we can't do it. The fire will blaze for about ten minutes and then die out. Not even a cinder will be left. Similarly, if we try and compete on just carbs, we will run out of fuel midway through the match when we need the energy the most, so we must work some fats into our tournament fuel plan. Complex carbs and good fats are how we keep our competitive bonfire roaring for an entire tournament.

Sugar Is Devastating

Sugars are part of the carb family, but not all sugars are created equal. We need to separate "natural" sugar from "refined" sugar. Refined sugars are everywhere. Refined sugars can be so devastating to competitive concentration, physical timing, and endurance that they deserve much closer attention.

POSER FOOD

Don't be a taste junky. Break free of flavor and convenience.
Adapt! Put in some effort and choose fresh rocketfuel over
low-energy poser food. Connect fueling to winning.

Sugary foods like donuts, candy bars, pastries, cookies, etc., and sugary
drinks like soda pop, sports drinks, energy drinks, etc., have no place in a
focused, winning competitor's diet—at all, ever!

• *Point: eliminate refined sugar.*

The energy from sugary foods and fluids enters the bloodstream too
quickly, almost as if injected by a syringe. We call this sugar dumping,
which is tied to poor decision-making and sloppy execution.

Sugary foods and fluids cause our blood sugar to rise too far above the
optimal level. When this happens, the pancreas secretes insulin, which pulls
the extra sugar out of the bloodstream to store it. Guess what happens next.
Yep, we crash. The insulin effect robs the available energy from our bloodstream, leaving us quickly depleted. Hence, we make poor decisions, display hesitant execution, and recovery is almost non-existent.

The deeper understanding here, as we discussed, is that our brain cannot store extra energy—it is totally dependent on a continuous new supply
from the bloodstream. When we dump sugar, soon after the insulin effect
takes hold, our brain goes into crisis mode. We feel weak, confused, spaced-

out, nervous, and indecisive, along with many other negative side effects. And it's all because of a taste-driven sugar craving.

• *Point: get off the Sugar-Train bound for Poor Performanceville.*

Review the high-octane *Big Dog Fuel Groups* examples on page 49, and limit yourself to those or similar choices. Think with your fierce Big Dog competition mindset first, not with your taste buds—if not every day, then at least throughout the season and especially before and during matches.

Liquid Sugar

Wow! Continuing with the sugar-is-devastating theme, realize that sugary sports drinks, energy drinks, soda pop, etc., are the worst offenders. All are liquid sugar delivery systems that crush performance. All are nothing but Little Dog taste comforters.

• *Point: Sugar is heroin. It's addictive, it's everywhere, and it's horrible!*

Reality check: For taste junkies this is challenging information. In other words, to keep the same (bad) food habits, taste junkies must reject this information. But *WinningSTATE* athletes take in challenging information, because they know that knowledge equals power and applying that knowledge leads to winning.

Despite what the companies who sell the variations of liquid sugar want us to believe, the stuff not only doesn't provide any benefit, but it also has a negative effect.

WATER

CARBS

FUELING SEQUENCE

Our decision making machine (our brain) needs a continuous supply of new fuel. Mute your taste buds! Make winning, high-performance fuel choices. No poser food. No sugar.

Sports-drink salespeople love to talk about electrolytes. (Have you seen the movie *Idiocracy*?) The claim of "optimally replenishing vital electrolytes and nutrients" is a marketing ploy to sell more drinks. Our bodies are 70% water, not 70% sugary drink. So when we've sweated off pounds of water, we need to replenish it with pure water. A simple multi-mineral tablet along with lots of water will do more than sports drinks for replenishing electrolytes, which prevent cramping and other important nerve/muscle functions.

Sayo.org added the following to this discussion: "Professional and college athletes drink water at their events, even though the water comes out of Gatorade jugs." (Notice what most winning coaches get doused with at the end of a game: ice and water.)

Just Google "replenish electrolytes" and you'll see what I'm talking about. Look for sources on the net that aren't trying to sell you something and you'll get the straight information.

An additional reason to stay away from man-made sugar drinks is the toxic chemicals. There is so much garbage in many of the liquid-sugar drinks like dyes, preservatives, etc., that our body has to work at discarding the garbage in order to use the water left behind.

CARB/FAT COMBO

One of the real dangers of trying to hydrate with liquid sugar is we become taste addicted and won't drink water, so we fail to hydrate as much as needed. Connect with the math in this example: In a hot, muggly gym we can easily sweat off several (two to four) pounds of fluid during a match. This makes hydrating with liquid sugar difficult; it's too concentrated and has too much junk in it. We instinctively stop hydrating after a couple of pounds. For full hydration we would need to drink one of the monster sports drink containers, the big one, the sixty-four-ounce one (four pounds). We won't do it and we'll be down two pounds of fluid, so dehydration sets in and by the end of the match we're confused, slow, and disoriented. Or, even if we are the type that will drink several pounds of liquid sugar, it's just as bad. The effect is still negative. Make sense?

• *Point: drink pure H₂O.*

The energy from fresh fruit (already explained) gets in our bloodstream quicker and burns better. Don't interpret eating a piece of fruit as drinking gallons of fruit juice. A large amount of fruit juice is not recommended; it's too acidic and will cause digestive issues. To be very clear, I'm not advocating hydrating with fruit juice. I'm suggesting eating a single piece of fruit before or after matches to keep our blood sugar level elevated—*hydrate with water.*

Tie fueling and hydrating choices to high-performance results, not mindless taste preferences. Think green, not machine. Think water, not liq-

FUEL with fresh, high-octane foods, forget about taste and convenience.

uid sugar. Think fresh carbs and good fats, along with skipping the protein before a match.

Proteins Are Wet Green Wood

At tournaments, proteins are not max energy sources. Proteins are like green wood on a fire—they don't burn quickly. The body uses proteins to rebuild muscle and other cells. It doesn't easily use proteins as gasoline (energy), so the protein just lies in our stomach taking up digestive capacity. Before and during a match is not the time to rebuild cells. Before and during a match is the time to fill our empty gas tank.

Protein is a good thing at night, when we're through practicing or competing for the day. In fact, when not competing, we need protein throughout the day for a variety of reasons. The primary sources of non-vegetarian protein are beef, poultry, and fish. Tuna is a great source of protein and other important nutrients (e.g., omega fats).

In case this isn't clear, before and during a competition: no protein and no sugar!

Fresh High-Octane Sources

High-octane sources of food and fluids come from nature. They're fresh, meaning alive, not dead. They haven't been processed or modified from their original states. If food has gone through a machine, and had anything taken from it or added to it, it's been processed. Processed food is dead, tongue food, not fresh, high-octane, mind-and-body performance fuel. Nature provides high-octane fuel for max energy. Machines do not.

Here's a simple test. You're on your way to practice and forgot to eat. You have the option to quickly breeze through a fast food drive-thru or to park and go inside a grocery store for some high-octane items. Which do you choose? Yes, grabbing packaged products is easier and they taste good.

That's because most packaged products are artificial, but artificial doesn't get the job done. For example: If our shoes weren't the real deal off the shelf and fell apart when we used them, would we buy them? No, we wouldn't. Someday food manufacturers will get it, but not until the majority of us stop buying the sugar-laced, toxic junk.

• *Point: choosing high-octane sometimes takes more effort, but then don't most things that produce a benefit?*

A large percentage of man-made processed products, like protein bars, have added ingredients. Preservatives have been added for longer shelf life and flavor enhancers have been added to excite our taste buds. This processing alters the structure of the food and makes it harder for our body to burn efficiently. The additives are another issue, but I won't go into how life-draining processed foods are, I'll just stay focused on their inability to be converted to high-octane fuel.

A positive note: Healthy snacks are on the rise. Some "bar" companies are making their products with organic (not processed and chemical free), pure ingredients.

Let your Big Dog out; make time to prepare meals and snacks for high-gear performances. Energy first, flavor second.

So if you like the convenience of bars, just do a little research and look at the ingredients list. Choose a brand that's made from natural ingredients: oats, fruit, peanut butter, etc. If you can't pronounce an ingredient, typically it's a man-made chemical. If you have to consume packaged products, buy ones that are both a great fuel source and good for you.

Another problem with most bars is they are very low in calories and extremely low in fat. That's a bad thing. Typically, most bars are around 200–230 calories with less than five grams of fat. For most of us that means about twenty minutes worth of medium-grade fuel, even if we choose a bar from natural, fresh sources. So, if we eat a bar just before a match with the idea that we're completely fueling up, we're wrong. Midway through we'll be out of gas, especially if our nerves are sparking. A wholegrain bagel and cream cheese, a wholegrain peanut butter and jelly sandwich, or nut mixes are much better choices than just a bar.

• *Point: choose fresh foods that are full fat—no low fat anything.*

The *Food Court* illustration back on pages 44 and 45 offers an exaggerated view of the poser food vs. rocket fuel debate. One side represents processed, dead junk food, while the other side represents fresh sources from nature. Burgers, fries, shakes, hot dogs, soda pop, chips with plastic cheese, and processed pizza from concession stands, along with quickie mart microwaveable anything, are not high-octane Big Dog fuel sources.

Clarification: burgers, fries, shakes, and pizza are not villains in and of themselves; it's the source of the ingredients that matters. A burger made

Choose foods that are high-octane fuel sources over foods that are processed for taste and convenience.

from lean organic beef, a wholegrain bun, fresh organic vegetables, and organic condiments is awesome. The same goes for pizza: wholegrain dough, organic sauce, free range meats, real cheese, fresh vegges, etc. Fries are great, if they're real, unprocessed potatoes deep-fried in premium oil. A shake is awesome, if it's from whole milk, real ice cream, fresh organic berries, minus the added sugar syrup.

• *Point: the source of the ingredients is the issue, not the type of food.*

Got the picture? Choose foods that are high-octane fuel sources over foods that are processed for taste and convenience. You can eat dead, toxic junk all year long if you want to—yuck! But I encourage you to consume mostly high-octane Big Dog fuel during the season. Look past your taste buds and think about what your mind and body need to recover from the extreme energy drain of long practices and intense competition.

Food choices are either powerful or weak, and since the choice is ours, let's choose powerful.

Tournament Fuel Plan

Put together a tournament fuel plan. Review the *3 Match Fuel Plan* on page 57. A three to five match tournament over a weekend obviously requires some advance fuel planning due to the quantity of fuel required. We eat and

BIG DOG "BONFIRE" FUEL CHOICES

Paper
Banana

Apple

Mixed Berries

Twigs
Wholegrain Bagels

Wholegrain Bread

Brown Rice

Oatmeal

Logs
Cream Cheese

Peanut Butter

Avocado

Mixed Nuts (Trail Mix)

Cheese Stick (Whole fat)

QUANTITY LIST:

- 3 pieces of fruit

- 3 bagels and cream cheese (or 3 PB&Js)

- 1 lb. of nut mix (no candy or chocolate)

- 3 pounds (48 oz) of water

H_2O VOLUME is significant, especially if you're playing in a hot, muggy arena.

3 MATCH FUEL PLAN

Do some planning and bring your Big Dog "Bonfire" fuel with you. Food choices are either powerful or weak, and since the choice is yours, choose powerful.

hydrate on schedule, we don't wait until we're hungry or thirsty. By then it would be too late.

A couple of hours before a match we grab a real piece of fruit: banana, orange, or apple. We consume this simple carb (paper), which immediately puts fuel in our tank; fruit quickly increases our blood sugar level and we feel instantly energized. We wash the piece of fruit down with water.

After the initial piece of fruit and H2O comes a carb/fat combo: a wholegrain bagel and cream cheese, or a wholegrain bagel and peanut butter, or a wholegrain peanut butter and jelly sandwich, plus a nut mix on the side. Stay away from meat (protein).

The amount of carb/fat combo we need depends on our size. If we're less than 150 pounds we may only need one serving, but if we're 150 pounds plus, we may need a couple. Add sparking nerves the morning of a match, we can easily consume too much too fast, making ourselves uncomfortable. After twenty minutes or so, we can go back for more if needed, but the second time we *skip the fruit*. We grab another carb/fat combo. Once we're full, there's probably an hour or so before starting warm-ups, so we put on our headphones, breathe, think about all of our Big Dog success, and let our body absorb the rocket fuel.

After warm-ups, we make sure to have premium snacks and water with us for easy access. We don't wait until we get hungry. By then our blood sugar will be down and our crispness, both physically and mentally, will be lessened. Fruit and nut mixes are great between sets. A piece of fruit and a couple of handfuls of nut mix with some water elevates and sustains our blood sugar level, enabling us to finish with a clear head. That's nut mixes minus the candy and chocolate of course—no sugar.

Late in the tournament we may need to snack every thirty minutes or so, especially during longer tournaments with a lot of matches. As we attack our way to the final match that decides who emerges the champion, we fuel with the purpose of sustaining excellent decision-making and powerful execution.

Additionally, resting is critical between matches. As soon as possible after finishing, we fuel up and *get horizontal* to start recuperating for the next match. Remember, resting is more for our mind and emotions than it is for our body.

Before tournaments, do some planning and some shopping, and bring the high-octane fuel items with you to build your competitive bonfire and keep it blazing through the entire tournament.

Bring It With You

I rarely see teams provide or require specific fuel items for their competitors, which is a bit of a mystery to me. If I were running the show, there would be ample quantities of high-octane fuel available during tournaments: fresh fruit, wholegrain bagels and cream cheese, wholegrain peanut butter and jelly sandwiches, nut mixes, and gallons of water.

Processed burgers, fries, and shakes are not optimal fuel sources. The plastic cheese, chips, and hot dogs at the concession stand aren't either.

If your team is not one that provides or requires specific fuel items, put it on your list of competition necessities and bring it with you. It's not that tough; throw some high-octane snacks and plenty of water in your sports bag. Make fueling part of your tournament process. Make smart choices that include fresh carbs and good fat.

Make Smart Choices

For outstanding performances during the season, we need to add some high-octane fuel to our daily and weekly food intake. It familiarizes our digestive system with dense-energy foods and helps us recover and rebuild more quickly during the week.

Another example of making smart choices relates to breakfast when we're out-of-town at away tournaments, especially title tournaments. We need to be careful (smart) about going to a restaurant for the *great* breakfast before the *big* match. Emotionally that sounds and feels good, but unless we've eaten that great breakfast at that particular restaurant before, it's not a good idea. We need to stay with what our body knows. Eating breakfast at an unfamiliar restaurant before a competition is *high risk*. We don't know what we're going to get.

If going to a restaurant is a must, we need to be smart about our choices. We need to eat with max energy in mind first and flavor second. Personally, I wouldn't even consider going to an unfamiliar restaurant the morning of a big match—*not a chance!*

As we close this chapter the key point is this: food manufacturers are not on our side, even though their advertising is trying to convince us that they are. They're playing us. They're taking advantage of our natural love for taste. But as high-performance athletes, we must get over it and make smarter choices, not uninformed flavor choices.

WinningSTATE athletes follow the thinking that competing mentally tough under pressure and getting it done requires high-performance fueling. *WinningSTATE* athletes think of food more functionally than emotionally, especially during the season. They think about what their mind and body need to be ready for the next match, not just what tastes good. Join the team. Make smart, winning food choices to fuel your fierceness.

Remember, tournaments are not the days to indulge our taste buds, save that for after the competition—a victory celebration dinner will taste even better.

Now you know how to *fuel your performance*—with fresh carbs and good fats.

POWER UP

3 FUEL

Don't be a taste junky. Choose fresh carbs and fats, hydrate with H_2O. Eliminate protein and sugar.

TOURNAMENT PROCESS

Gather your paper, twigs, and logs, plus H_2O.

FOCUS POINT

Fuel and hydrate frequently or run out of gas.

THE BIG 3

SELF-TALK

"I need to fuel for performance, not eat for taste."

VISUALIZE

Picture your 3 match fuel plan.

ADAPT

Eat to win! Consume rocketfuel, not poser food.

WinningSTATE
The Mental Toughness Company

4 ANTICIPATE
LOVE THE NERVES

How do nerves affect you? Do you hate nerves or do you love nerves? Nerves are not the enemy, doubt is the enemy. *WinningSTATE* athletes anchor their self-belief by responding with a level head ("Of course I'm nervous"), and then riding the adrenaline into battle.

R espond! Don't just react. Become skilled at *anticipating* the nerves.

If we can't *ANTICIPATE* our nervous reactions to performing in public, how can we expect to handle the adrenaline? We can't. Nervy moments will always be part of competing, some moments more intense than others. But during every go-time, nervy moment the adrenaline hits and scatters our thinking, we must be able to anticipate the nerves and respond—inside!

If we can't anticipate and positively respond, nerves turn into doubt, and, uncontested, doubt cuts the legs right out from under us. A hostile environment, a go-time situation, and the Superwoman juice all combine to create that super-charged, highly volatile athletic experience. If we can't skillfully ride the adrenaline (yeehaw!) and control what's going on in our head, to put it nicely, we underachieve. In extreme cases we turn into spaghetti, get desperate, melt down emotionally, make poor decisions, and hand the match to our opponents.

Every competitive athlete has experienced a catastrophic meltdown at one time or another. We get a certain look, almost like we're in shock.

"Toughen up! Face the nerves head-on and use the Superwoman juice to your advantage."

Our eyes glaze over and we don't respond well to conversation. We become distant, confused, and disoriented because we haven't equipped ourselves with the skills to *anticipate the nerves*, respond with a level head, and have some fun.

Yes! Have some fun! Has dreading the outcome ever produced anything productive? No, it hasn't. And it never will.

WinningSTATE athletes, whether attackers or protectors, face their primal competitive reaction to performing in public head-on. They mentally train to harness the Superwoman juice and use it to their advantage. *WinningSTATE* athletes turn themselves inside out before the spotlight does. They figure out their primal reactions to pressure so they can positively respond and fight back rather than passively surrendering and giving in. We all must become skilled at anticipating the nerves.

Our Primal Competitive Reaction

Nerves are not the enemy. Apprehension and doubt are the enemy. Nerves are a good thing. Nerves produce adrenaline, and to harness the adrenaline we must understand our primal competitive reaction to pressure of any kind: Do we fight, flee, or freeze?

Take a look at the *Fight, Flee, or Freeze* illustration on page 65. Ask yourself, "What is your primal competitive reaction? Do you fight, flee, or freeze, and to what degree?" To fight is to face confrontation head-on and fiercely battle; to flee is to completely avoid confrontation and run away; to freeze is to be so petrified we neither fight nor flee, but freeze and get run over.

Yes, this is a squirmy topic, but we can't stick our head in the sand. Mentally tough competitors (*WinningSTATE* athletes) know their primal competitive reaction like the backs of their hands. In other words, we must know our basic reaction to nerves so we can control ourselves on the battleground. Those who hide from the truth don't adapt or evolve, so they never learn how to handle the nerves. We must toughen up and evaluate. We don't avoid evaluating our physical skills, right? We must also evaluate our Grr Factor—our primal competitive reaction to nerves.

• *Point: we must toughen up and face the nerves head-on.*

WinningSTATE athletes have an advantage because they separate posturing from reality. To explain the difference: Some of us act (posture) like we're Big Dogs, but when confrontation gets in our face, we crumble and crash. Or we act like an "average guy," but when we cross paths with confrontation, we step up and let our Big Dog out; we don't flee or melt down. *WinningSTATE* athletes realize that posturing is acting and acting doesn't get the job done. Make sense?

We humans are wired in a predetermined way to instantly react to danger, just like animals.

To help the process of turning yourself inside out put yourself in the following scene. Pretend you're playing in a televised match where the TV cameras are on your every move. The commentators are describing your conviction for every shot you make. What would the TV cameras capture? What would the commentators be saying about you? How would they describe your execution? Not your physical technique—your Grr Factor. That's how we need to view ourselves, which is reality, not posturing.

Now take that realistic, personal, turn-you-inside-out Grr Factor assessment and picture the Grr Meter and where you naturally fit. How do you typically react to confrontation? Relax, nobody will know your honest evaluation unless you want them to. But it's important that you know, because insight reveals weaknesses in our mental game and turning weaknesses into strengths equals power—*competitive power.*

Let's look at our primal competitive reaction to confrontation from a different angle. We humans are wired in a predetermined way to instantly react to danger, just like animals. This is our self-preservation reaction, which we discussed earlier. However, what sets us humans apart from the rest of the animal kingdom is the ability to recognize and alter those primal predispositions. We can *choose* whether we fight, flee, or freeze, and to what degree. Yes, responding to our primal reactions is complex and difficult, but

| FIGHT | FLEE | FREEZE |

FIGHT, FLEE OR FREEZE

How does pressure affect you? Do you fight, flee or freeze?
Evaluate your primal competitive reaction, so you can anticipate
the nerves and respond with a level head.

we must figure it out if we want to win consistently. If a Navy SEAL recruit can't figure out how to control his nerves, he's out. It's the same for competitive athletes.

We all have the intestinal fortitude to fiercely control our nerves. Remember the Grandma story? Our intestinal fortitude has absolutely nothing to do with our physical size or how naturally assertive we are. Fiercely controlling our nerves and taking action is a choice.

• *Point: where we fit on the Grr Meter—terrified to fuming—is up to us.*

Those who are naturally more aggressive probably have an advantage, but only while they're kids. Once the naturally hesitant realize that controlling their nerves is strictly about attitude and attitudes are a personal choice, everything changes—they take control, get some backbone, show some teeth, let their Big Dog out, and ride the adrenaline like a champ. That's what we want most of all, the self-belief that we can face the pressure, stand firm, and execute.

Think about it. We never earn respect just by winning. We earn respect by fighting back, by never giving up, by being *mentally tough* and giving it everything we've got.

President Dwight D. Eisenhower put it well: "It's not about the size of the dog in the fight; it's about the size of the fight in the dog."

Can't you see those competitive archetypes represented on the *Grr Meter* on page 67 in your life? Both behavioral extremes are represented, those who are paralyzed by hesitation as well as those who are out-of-control with anger. Both types have detrimental *primal behaviors* that require assertive control to perform well in competition. Typically, the naturally aggressive go over the top, while the naturally hesitant don't show up; aggressors underestimate their opponents, while hesitators overestimate their opponents; aggressors are shocked when they lose, while hesitators are shocked when they win. Very few competitors have trained themselves to anticipate, respond, and maintain a neutral or +1 attitude to gut-twisting apprehension.

• *Point: we must train to harness the raw primal energy rather than automatically allowing it to be overwhelming.*

A key point when considering this handling the nerves equation is that it's not the same for everyone. It's not one size fits all; it's very individual and personal. The nervous emotion associated with performing in public can be absolute dread for some, but for others it's exciting. Ask yourself, "Do you hate the nerves or do you love the nerves?" Obviously those who find performing in public exciting have an advantage because nerves are a reality competitive athletes must live with for their entire careers. Intimidation, distraction, confusion, doubt, hesitation, the potential of embarrassment, and a hundred other negative descriptors will always be part of a performance athlete's psyche; it's just the way it is, which is why a solid mental game is fundamental to winning.

• *Point: to perform well in public, you gotta love the nerves.*

You Gotta Love The Nerves

I bet you've heard the following phrase many times, as it's very common in sports culture to say, "You gotta love the spotlight." We've modified that phrase to "You gotta love the nerves."

| Terrified | Panicked | Tweaked | | Fierce | Angry | Fuming |

⌄ ANTICIPATE

Love the nerves. Respond. Breathe. Ride the adrenaline.
Give yourself a why-you-can-believe pep talk. Concentrate!
Be your own BFF.

Where do you think the term "adrenaline junkie" comes from, and why do you think billions of fans around the world love watching high-stakes competition? The nerves! The adrenaline! We love watching to see who can ride the lightning and who can't. Who can harness the Superwoman juice and use it vs. who gets consumed by it.

Here's what Rich Lerner of the Golf Channel had to say about Ricky Fowler: "He likes when the lights are real bright. He likes when the pressure is amped up. He's not afraid to step into the spotlight and let 'er rip."

That does not describe most of us, nor will it ever. If we don't naturally love to show off and be the center of attention, it's very difficult to create that deep down desire. The "idea" of learning to love being the center of attention is powerful, of course. If it were attainable it'd be a game changer, but most of us will never love the scrutiny or intensity of the spotlight. However, what all of us can do is learn to "love the nerves." All of us can evaluate and understand our predicable, repetitive reaction to pressure. Then we can anticipate and deliberately respond with mental toughness and a level head. *WinningSTATE* athletes love the nerves, because it's like plugging into an electric outlet. *WinningSTATE* athletes love the Superwoman juice.

When that raw power is pumping through our body, we can't be afraid of it or run away from it. We must do the opposite. We must welcome it and run to it. We must admit we're slightly nervous, freaked out, scared to death, whatever the case may be, so we can face the pressure head-on, get that wry smile, and go for it. We must love the rush and have some fun. We say to ourselves, "Of course I'm nervous, I'm in a tournament and don't want to look bad. Get a grip, take a breath, and focus on SMS." Sort of a "duh" moment—this is what we do, we're competitors.

To ride the lightning we must give ourselves factual, realistic reasons why we can succeed. In other words, when we feel that lump in our throat, we use our counterarguments to talk ourselves down from the competitive-suicide ledge. We use this metaphor because "jumpers" can be *talked down* from a pessimistic, doom-and-gloom state. We must be able to do the same for ourselves. We must be able to *coach ourselves up* to an optimistic, winning, love-the-nerves state of mind. This levelheaded self-talk process is fueled with facts: our

> ## To ride the lightening we must give ourselves factual, realistic reasons why we can succeed.

strengths, our past success, and no-nonsense reasons why we can succeed at that moment. Our self-talk conversation looks something like this: "Whatever! It's just another set. I've got skills and I'm ready for a fight. Who cares who's watching? That's what crowds do, watch. So watch this!" Get the idea? We coach ourselves up with The Big 3.

In the next two chapters we talk much more about our self-talk counterarguments and drawing competitive power (self-belief) from the mental pictures of our past Big Dog success. For now, realize that all of us must adapt. We must know what to expect from ourselves under the lights. Then, after facing our primal reactions we can say, "Yeah...this is usually where I puke," then laugh it off, switch attitudes, narrow our focus, Grr up, and use the adrenaline to our advantage.

• *Point: we must positively respond, have some fun, and ride the lightning!*

WinningSTATE Adrenaline Routines

Building a mental game is much broader than just mental preparation. The term "preparation" is so limiting. As performance athletes, we do a lot more than just prepare mentally, we also execute mentally. We use the five

Little Dog   Big Dog

NERVY SITUATIONS

Nervy situations are endless. Crushing apprehension is a constant battle. In sports, the classroom, and social situations mental toughness is required to respond, believe, and take action.

WinningSTATE Adrenaline Routines—plan, fuel, rest, breathe, and re-hearse—to get our mind into mental toughness mode, both before and during a competition. We plan for our competition necessities, we make sure to have plenty of high-octane fuel, we rest as much as possible, we breathe slowly and deeply, and we rehearse SMS. Let's break down the five Adrenaline Routines.

ANTICIPATE the nerves and respond with a level head. Face the pressure head on.

#1 Plan:

Before matches and tournament weekends, especially before leaving for an away competition, planning and packing *all* of our competition necessities is critical. First, we make a list—a written list. Then we make sure all our things are laid out in front of us and ready to be packed: equipment, back-up equipment, clothes, high-octane fuel and H2O, accessories, etc.

Example: If we want specific clothes for after the tournament, we list them and pack them. If we want specific music for the ride there and while we're in the stands, we list it and pack it. If we have favorite gear: shoes, shorts, headband, wristbands, kneepads or anything special that helps us handle the nerves and believe, we make sure it's listed and checked off in our bag. Whatever is important to us, we list it, pack it, and check it.

This may seem trivial, but it's not. For the big shows we need to make ourselves as psychologically comfortable as possible and our *things* help accomplish that.

- *Point: a comfortable pre-tournament routine is what we're after.*

Why put out the extra effort to write out a list? When there are a lot of items to organize and we don't want to forget anything critical, a list provides added assurance. So instead of thinking about what we might have left behind, we can stay in the pre-tournament moment and think about stuff that matters, like facing the nerves head-on, picturing our Big Dog attacker or protector attitude, preparing specific SMS thoughts and detailing our job at each of the 3 Battle Zones.

Little Dogs, your mother is not your list.

We don't pack our bags until we've gathered everything in a group in front of us and can check things off as we pack. Planning and being organized and meticulous about packing our competition necessities not only makes sure we'll have everything we want and need at the competition, but the process also puts our mind in a poised and focused place—a narrow, in the moment, competition mindset. Planning helps increase our sense of control.

#2 Fuel:

Chapter 3 must have convinced you that *nutrition cannot be ignored*, especially for the big, multi-match tournaments. Now it's time to make fueling a standard "routine" that's part of your tournament process.

First, let's do a quick review. Bring that bonfire metaphor to mind. We want clean-burning, high-octane, quick-recovery fuel: fresh fruit, whole grains, and good fats. Not weak, low-energy food imposters: candy, burgers, hot dogs, chips, plastic cheese, and colored sugar-water, just to name a few. Remember, *fats* are the most important fuel for our competitive fire, and any kind of refined sugar can be devastating to our high-performance competitive machine.

Item by item, choose your Big Dog fuel regime. What's your favorite fruit preference? What about wholegrain: bread, bagel, or pasta? Or, are you more of a brown rice or vegetable person? What type of fat? Peanut butter (not hydrogenated—the kind we have to stir), cream cheese, avocado, or a nut mix? Do you know where these items are located in the grocery store? Plan out the quantity of high-octane fuel needed, and H2O, and make sure you have it ready to go.

Not only do we want to be well fueled and fully recovered before and after each match, we want to be as comfortable as possible and proper fueling and maximum hydration helps that considerably. A full gas tank puts our mind at ease and helps us rest.

#3 Rest:

During a competition, resting, like fueling, is more for our mind and our nerves than it is for our body. The mental strain of grappling with apprehension and physically recovering over numerous matches of a big tournament is very draining and requires frequent resting and refueling. During a tournament, figuring out how and when to take rest breaks between matches is vital to stringing together one mentally crisp, well-executed shot after the next.

"There is only one way to achieve success. It is to take charge of your mind."

Eric Butterworth

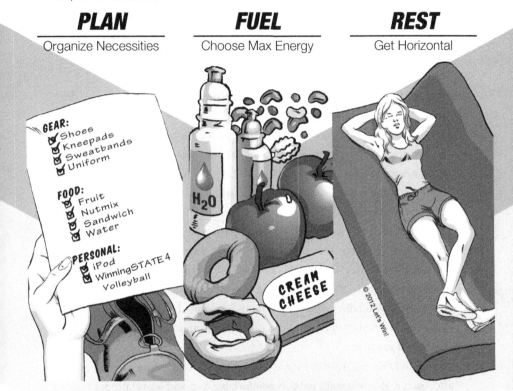

PLAN
Organize Necessities

FUEL
Choose Max Energy

REST
Get Horizontal

GEAR:
☑ Shoes
☑ Kneepads
☑ Sweatbands
☑ Uniform

FOOD:
☑ Fruit
☑ Nutmix
☑ Sandwich
☑ Water

PERSONAL:
☑ iPod
☑ WinningSTATE 4
   Volleyball

H₂O

CREAM CHEESE

© 2012 Let's Win!

ADRENALINE ROUTINES

Make the Adrenaline Routines part of your tournament
process to take charge of the nerves and put your mind into
a winning state. Work your mental game.

Think about it—how many other activities in our life require intense
concentration for several hours straight? Typically none. Expecting our
brain to function at a high level for an entire tournament without frequently
resting and refueling is like trying score well on the SATs after cramming all
night and not eating an energy-packed breakfast. It's not gonna happen. Being able to concentrate under pressure at both ends of the court, match after
match requires deliberate rest breaks throughout a tournament.

• *Point: we must get horizontal at least 50% of the time!*

Well, that's if the arena has bleachers, not seats. Bleachers allow us to
bring a sleeping bag and pillow to get horizontal and chill out. We stake out

BREATHE
Slow & Deep

Nose - In
3-5 sec

Hold
2 sec

Hold
2 sec

Mouth - out
3-5 sec

REHEARSE
Focus Points

our territory, put on some music, and relax, meaning we disengage from people and commotion. Check out the *Rest* illustration on page 72. Horizontal is best. Think about it. When we're really tired, what do we want to do? We want to lie down. Or somehow close our eyes and rest our head.

Why is horizontal best? No gravity. Picture your heart and circulatory system. When does our heart have the easiest time, when we're standing or lying down? When we're lying down. If the venue has seats we must figure out the best way to close our eyes and let our body go limp. Sleeping bags and pillows still help the resting process, even in seats. They help us get comfortable, which helps us rest. The point is, find a place, stake out your territory, and sprawl out. At tournaments we can't be afraid of falling asleep between matches. Getting horizontal for forty minutes does wonders, and if we can actually fall asleep for twenty of those minutes it's even better. We will have plenty of time to get ourselves up and ready for the next match.

• *Point: falling asleep is a good thing, so lie down and chill out!*

Language note: If "rest" seems too much like going to bed or taking a nap, and it doesn't make sense to rest and compete at the same time, give the routine a different name: regroup, power-up, refocus, whatever works for you—just make sure you disengage from people and commotion by getting horizontal. And get lots of air—breathe!

#4 Breathe:

Increased oxygen, along with physically controlling the inhale/exhale process has such a positive, measured effect on our nerves under pressure that we made competitive breathing a formal routine. We use our competitive breathing routine both before and during a competition, so plan on becoming skilled at deep, competitive breathing. Most likely it will become one of your most commonly used *WinningSTATE* mental toughness routines.

Oxygen is one of those gotta-have kinds of things, so learning how to breathe as we're strangling ourselves is very useful. The increased oxygen is calming and the physically rhythmic part induces an active sense of control that translates into greater self-control overall. This deep, competitive breathing skill can be performed almost anywhere: sitting, standing, leaning, or lying down—in through your nose, out through your mouth. Slowly and steadily control the air flowing in and out, holding at each end.

Pause and study the *Breathe* figures on page 73. Slowly inhale through your nose and as your lungs get to the full point, take in a little more. Then hold for three to five seconds. Purposely and slowly exhale through your mouth. Don't rush the exhale. Control the flow all the way to the last bit of air, then push out a little more. Now the really challenging part: don't gasp to take in a breath. Not even a quick little breath. Start inhaling slowly through your nose until your lungs are full again, which should take between three to five seconds. Hold when full, don't rush the exhale. Exhaling takes about the same amount of time as inhaling. Three to five seconds in both directions—the slower the better. Then repeat the cycle. Controlling the start of inhaling and exhaling is the tough part. At first you'll want to gasp for air (and probably will). That's okay. It's just a reflex that, once controlled, yields big benefits.

For example: The night before a tournament, when the nerves start sparking, we sit back, close our eyes and purposefully engage some deep, competitive breathing to calm down. Or, we might be thinking about an upcoming match or dominant opposing player. We see ourselves in fierce Big Dog execution mode, but right along with that positive vision are negative "what if I blow it" scenarios. To stay on the positive track, we kick in some breathing, take the Doubt Demons by the neck, and quiet them down.

Competitive breathing is truly amazing, after several in-and-out cycles you'll feel relaxed and energized at the same time. The deep, competitive breathing skill is a very effective tool for many emotionally charged situations. Learn how to breathe, so you can focus and fight back.

• *Point: we use competitive breathing to engage SMS and our job at each battle zone.*

#5 Rehearse:

Rehearsing is just another name for practice, and in the mental world that simply means thinking about doing something, turning it over in our mind.

Drilling physical skills is a form of rehearsing. We must drill our mental skills as well. Rehearsing performing in public familiarizes us with those uncomfortable feelings of being center stage. The more we think about handling the nerves productively, the more we're able to love the nerves when it's go-time.

Visualize it. See yourself in a competition against formidable opponents and hundreds of fans. Visualize being center stage and feel the nervous energy from the crowd's "all eyes on you" attention. Actually turn and face the spectators. In other words, face the pressure head-on.

Doubt triggers are nasty; rehearse dealing with all the hesitant thoughts and feelings that predictably erupt when it's showtime. Rehearse your switch ritual, your customized SMS Sequence, and your job at each of the 3 Battle Zones. Make sense? This is what building a mental game is all about—thinking!

This is why mental toughness skill building is so much more than just mental preparation. We're rehearsing our counterarguments to focus on during the match. The cool thing about mental rehearsal, unlike drilling

"The ultimate measure of a woman ... is where she stands at times of challenge and controversy."
Martin Luther King, Jr.

physical skills, is that we can do it anywhere: on the bus, in the car, in the stands, on the bench, lying in bed at night, etc. We can rehearse recalling our past Big Dog success and grounding our self-talk in left-brain "been there, done that" facts anywhere. We train ourselves to be mentally active before the match, so we can be mentally on point during the match.

Chapters 5 and 6 will dig deeper into rehearsing the *WinningSTATE* key mental toughness skills and routines, both before and during a competition. For now, realize that the more familiar and prepared we are for the emotional rollercoaster of nerve-racking competition, the better we're able to ride it.

Tackle The Nerves Head-On

Welcome the enemy. Welcome the butterflies, the doubt, and the apprehension—learn to love the nerves! In other words, smile inside, stop dwelling on possible negative outcomes, and have some fun.

Here's a personal doubt story. In 1983 I was competing in the US Senior National Powerlifting Championships, which at the time was the most competitive tournament of the year, even more competitive than the world championships.

I lifted in the 181-pound weight class and was in the best shape of my career. In a powerlifting competition the squat is the first lift. I was planning on attempting a personal record, which at the time was only a few pounds off of the world record.

In powerlifting you get three attempts on platform; the first two are basically warm-ups. When your name is called you have three minutes to execute the lift or you're disqualified. My first attempt in the squat at 644 pounds was easy. My second attempt at 683 pounds was incredibly solid. I felt great. I picked 722 pounds for my third and final attempt.

Nationals were being held in a huge arena with a few thousand people attending. As I walked on and took control of the platform I was in a great place mentally. I was completely doubt-free—or so I thought. As I ducked under the bar a little voice from Demon Land said, "You're going to fail," and along with the negative voice came this imaginary video of me taking the weight out of the rack, my legs breaking off at the knees, and the weight driving me straight down through the platform.

This obviously broke my concentration. I looked up and actually laughed out loud. It startled me, and it came from nowhere. I backed away from the weight, took several deep, purposeful breaths and told the little demon voice where to go. As I approached the bar the second time I fought back the negativity with real mental pictures from my solid warm-ups and numerous memories of successful big lifts in the past. Doubt resurfaced slightly, but Grred up and focused, I plowed ahead. I made the lift and in doing so set an Oregon state record that still stands today.

What's the moral of the story? Apprehension, doubt, and intimidation will surface at the worst possible time. Being able to deal with the emotional turbulence during critical moments is how

A mentally tough competitor looks intimidation square in the face, smiles, and says, "Oh yeah, watch this!"

we deliver clutch performances. A mentally tough competitor has the skills and core self-belief to look intimidation square in the face, smile, and say, "Oh yeah, watch this!"

Even though our genetic cocktail has an influence over how we react to confrontation, we can change that reaction if we don't avoid evaluating how pressure affects us. When we toughen up and evaluate our primal competitive reaction to pressure, we're able to *anticipate the nerves* and then positively respond by taking control of our emotional state.

We must adapt! We must see our competitive emotions, the apprehension, the butterflies, the nervousness, the intimidation, etc., in a new light. We must get real and face the fact that nerves are unavoidable. Because thinking that someday we'll progress to the point where nerves won't be an issue is a mistake. The task is to see nerves differently, as raw, powerful energy that is neither positive nor negative, but neutral— a source of raw power that is completely natural and ours to do with as we please. The great thing is, when we're mentally skilled and can get out of our own way and use the Superwoman juice we all have in competition, our physical skills take over. That state is often referred to as "the zone," where crisp execution feels effortless; it's an incredible experience we never forget. But, if we can't anticipate the nerves and then positively respond our apprehensive Little Dog takes control and we will never find the zone.

Remember, we don't need to "love the spotlight," but we do need to learn how to "love the nerves." All of us can evaluate and understand our predicable, repetitive reaction to pressure. Then we can *anticipate* and deliberately respond with mental toughness and a level head. *WinningSTATE* athletes love the nerves. They love the Superwoman juice, because it's like plugging into an electric outlet.

As we close this chapter the key point is that we must tackle the nerves head-on to have a greater sense of control over our state of mind as we step into any competitive environment. We replace apprehensive *doubter reactions* with assertive *believer responses*. We smile inside and welcome the nerves, then we step up mentally tough and let our mind and body do what we've trained so hard to do—play tough and never give up.

Now you know how to *anticipate the nerves*—respond—and use the Superwoman juice to your advantage.

LOVE THE NERVES

4 ANTICIPATE

Don't let nerves get the best of you. Toughen up and respond—use the Superwoman juice.

TOURNAMENT PROCESS

Get ready to be nervous. Use the Adrenaline Routines.

FOCUS POINT

Anticipate your primal competitive reaction.

THE BIG 3

SELF-TALK

"Of course I'm nervous, get a grip and focus on SMS."

VISUALIZE

Picture conquering doubt by breathing and Grring up.

ADAPT

Have the mindset to respond to your PCR. Have fun!

WinningSTATE
The Mental Toughness Company

5 REPLACE
DRAW ON SUCCESS

How gripping is apprehension? Does it bind and shackle you or do you break free and go for it? WinningSTATE athletes free themselves of apprehension by concentrating. They counteract hesitant emotions by focusing on their Big Dog highlight reel.

C rush apprehension! Become skilled at replacing doubt with past success. If we can't bravely *REPLACE* apprehension and doubt with self-belief and conviction, we falter under pressure. When apprehension gains tsunami proportions, *WinningSTATE* athletes skillfully shift their focus to their personal Big Dog highlight reel.

Hold up here. Big Dog success is not just when we get the point or win the match. Do you remember discussing this previously? Big Dog success is also when we break free of apprehension in any situation and go for it. We must win mentally before we can win physically.

Doing anything in front of a crowd forces most of us out of our social comfort zone; our nerves explode and often paralyze us right on the spot. We retreat, rather than advance. But when we muster the courage and push through the apprehension and nervous negativity and go for it, that's when we win.

This definition of "Big Dog success" is so important to get our minds around, because overcoming apprehension is the objective, not squashing or suppressing the nerves. No matter how "confident" we are. No mat-

"Build your personal highlight reel. Vividly remember breaking free of apprehension and going for it."

ter how fierce our personality may be. No matter how well we may have prepared physically. Everyone, there are no exceptions, gets a lump in the throat before stepping into the public spotlight. It's natural. Our self-preservation reaction kicks in and we get apprehensive. Some of us push though that apprehensive feeling fairly easily, others not so easily, and still others are shackled and immobilized by it.

• *Point: All of us are encumbered by apprehension to some degree. The infamous "zone" is when we're free of apprehension, distractions, and doubt, and are 100% believing in ourselves.*

As performance athletes, apprehension is the "feeling" we must understand and conquer. This is why confidence is overrated. Mental toughness is what's needed to succeed on the battlefield, not feeling good about ourselves. Mental toughness skills are what we use to deal with nonstop apprehensive reactions.

Let's look at the definition of apprehension, along with several synonyms. ap-pre-hen-sion: fear over what may happen, sometimes escalating to dread. Synonyms: concern, uneasiness, worry, hesitation, indecision, panic, and dread.

Apprehension stops us in our tracks if we can't seize that feeling and push past it. When we overcome the nervous apprehension and go for it, that's the winning part. The ultimate outcome is irrelevant. Sometimes we make the play, sometimes we don't. Either way, when we suck it up and break free of our better sense of safety and leap, that's when we win. We must first assess our performances, not based on whether we stick a serve or smash a kill shot, but based on whether we show up mentally, handle the emotions, and get the job done. We defined getting the job done as we execute. When we skillfully ride the adrenaline and *intelligently* give it everything we've got, that's a Big Dog victory!

Think of it this way: If we execute our game plan to the best of our ability, what more can we ask of ourselves? There is nothing more we can ask, which is why it's a Big Dog victory.

• *Point: breaking free of apprehension and executing with conviction is our success, our Big Dog success.*

For some of us, getting our mind around winning without medaling is a stretch. But this perspective is worth grappling with. Here are some additional examples of when we get apprehensive: speaking in front of a group, taking a test, asking someone out, addressing a confrontational situation at home, school, or work. Some of us get apprehensive before we go out socially, some of us get nervous before practice, and most of us get apprehensive every time we step onto the court. The list goes on and on.

We argue that when we learn to recognize those apprehensive reactions in our everyday life and make the connection that those feelings are the same feelings we get in competition, just amplified, we're better able to (1) understand the feelings that hold us back, (2) fight those feelings and turn the energy into an advantage, and (3) draw genuine self-belief from all of our breaking-free-from-apprehension experiences.

This self-checking feeling we call apprehension is what we must understand and conquer to be able to step into the competitive spotlight, use the Superwoman juice, and execute with conviction.

Keep an Active/Open Mind

"Minds are like parachutes, they only work when they're open."

—Sir James Dewar, Scientist

Be curious. Keep an active/open mind. Constantly replace old, worn-out information and habits with new, more evolved ways of thinking and training to succeed in high-stakes sports. Construct your tournament process to bring order to the chaos, and rapidly build mentally tough concentration points to anchor your self-belief. Adapt!

THE SPOTLIGHT

Break free of apprehension, doubt, and poor performances.
Breathe, narrow, replace. Work your mental game to step
into the spotlight and deliver.

COMPETITION

Hope

Breathe   Narrow   Replace

Before we walk through a two-step process to highlight and vividly re-member our Big Dog victories (opposite page), let's talk about two common methods that attempt to deal with nerve-racking pressure: visualization and positive mental attitude (PMA). We want to make sure the differences be-tween those two methods and the *WinningSTATE* replace skill are crystal clear.

Visualization & PMA

Visualization and PMA have variations, so the following descriptions are broad. The most common form of visualization, not the *WinningSTATE* ver-sion, is to imagine what we want to have happen. The premise is that if we can visualize what we want to have happen physically when it's show-time and our brains are scrambled, we just plug into that vision and muscle memory will take over. The other common method to handle nerves and pressure-induced doubt is PMA, which is repeating positive statements, at-tempting to convince ourselves we're not really nervous.

Yes, I'm oversimplifying, but when we break down the two methods those basic descriptions are accurate.

I never had much success handling intense competitive pressure with either of those common methods, because they don't get at the root of the problem. We all get nervous (intimidated) to some degree when perform-ing in public and always will. Hesitant, destructive thinking must be faced head-on, dealt with and replaced, not ignored, avoided, or wished away. We must look the dragon directly in the eyes and fight back, not close our eyes, cover our ears, and tell ourselves the dragon doesn't exist.

Common visualization and PMA are not a complete set of handle-the-nerves skills, but they can be somewhat productive. Visualizing different offensive and defensive plays, our swing mechanics, timing, etc., is produc-tive. It's a useful mental activity that gives our mind something to do rather than dwell on what might go wrong. And repeating positive statements is always positive. But riding our right brain's negative molten lava without melting takes a greater skillset than imagining or repeating. It takes mental toughness and levelheaded thinking.

• *Point: replacing doubt with past success provides more believability than visu-alizing victory or repeating positive affirmations.*

Riding a bike
You may not remember learning to ride a bike, but can't you envision it and feel the fear? You did it anyway.

A diving board
Jumping off of anything in front of a crowd is intimidating. Imagine what the kids waiting were saying, "Come on, chicken!"

Fund raising
Stepping out from the group behind you with a request is scary. But we push forward and do it anyway.

Snowboarding
Taking off with a "yeehaw" takes guts and levelheaded thinking because our right brain is screaming "Don't do it!"

A dance
The possibility of rejection and humiliation is extreme, there's no way around it, but we toughen up and go for it.

BIG DOG VICTORIES

Our Big Dog victories are only when we feel apprehensive and doubtful, but despite the nerves we go for it. These brave responses to challenges start early in life. What are yours?

We must grasp the difference between trying to trick ourselves into thinking there's nothing to be afraid of vs. coaching ourselves up to deal with ever present apprehension and doubt. Instead of avoiding the nerves, we engage them head on and can calm ourselves down by intelligently replacing hesitant feelings with our past success.

Calming ourselves down (handling nerves) is largely dependent on how our memory is weighted. Is our memory weighted negatively or positively? In other words, which memories of dominate the front of our mind? Memories of underachieving or memories of performing well? If it's mostly negative we must forcefully shift our focus to remembering more Big Dog success, so we can draw on those been there, done that experiences under pressure.

We all have a fierce Big Dog attitude deep inside, we are all equipped with the ability to concentrate, and all of us can break free of our primal reactions to nerves. So every one of us can influence which memories, positive or negative, dominate our thinking. Believing positive or believing negative is a thought choice. So choose positive and believe it. Nike says, "If you have a body, you're an athlete." *WinningSTATE* says, "If you can think, you're a competitor."

Influencing Our Memory Scale

Pause and study the *Memory Scale* illustrations on pages 86 and 89. The figures on the negative side represent experiences when we didn't handle the nerves, while the experiences on the positive side represent when we did handle the nerves. Flip back and forth. Each figure represents an actual experience, not a fantasy.

How can we draw on success under pressure if we don't believe we've had any? Determining whether our memory is weighted negatively or positively is critical. A startling fact is that most of us remember mostly negative, not positive. Also, most of us have a tendency to overdramatize the slightest negative experience—blowing it totally out of proportion. But, since we all have both types of experiences, the goal is to remember our Big Dog victories in vivid detail.

NEGATIVE MEMORIES

If our Memory Scale is weighed negatively we're dominated by apprehensive, doubtful reactions. We must skillfully outweigh the negative to believe under pressure.

• *Point: Ask yourself if you recall and focus on mostly negative, crash-and-burn experiences or positive, get-it-done experiences?*

Here's another mental activity to help determine which memories dominate our thinking: negative or positive. If we had to make a list of ten negative personal attributes and ten positive, which list would be easier to complete? My guess is for most of us the negative list would fill up fast, but the positive list would be a struggle. Am I right?

What we remember and focus on is a choice—it's a learned mental activity. So we must train ourselves to focus on our positive experiences. The following may seem unnecessary, but let's better define both types of experiences to make sure the differences are crystal clear.

Our negative experiences are the easiest to understand. Most of us remember when we hesitate and crumble under pressure, when our thoughts and feelings are apprehensive and we crash. Our negative experiences are marked by pessimism, doubt, fear, confusion, and hesitation—a total lack of self-belief.

Our positive experiences are the complete opposite. Most of us don't remember when we toughen up, push through the apprehension, and go for it. For some odd reason most of us don't remember when we say to ourselves. "I can do this," and we succeed. Our positive experiences are marked by optimism, assertiveness, composure, clarity of focus, and conviction—a genuine doubt-free self-belief.

Keep in mind, without scary pressure—real intimidation—followed by recovery and execution, there's no Big Dog victory. An assertive Big Dog victory is only when we face an emotional challenge head-on, coach ourselves up, push through the nerves, and execute.

The task, and for most of us it's a difficult task, is remembering when we overcome apprehension and win—inside. When we take a breath, suck it up, take a risk, and go for it. Make sense? That's when we feel somewhat fulfilled, no matter the outcome. Deep down we know we didn't back down

POSITIVE MEMORIES

When our Memory Scale is weighted positively we're dominated by Big Dog "I can do this" thinking and feelings. We're optimistic, powerful, and courageous.

REPLACE apprehension, doubt, and hesitation with past Big Dog success.

during that apprehensive, nervy moment. Down deep we know we gave it everything we had. Our assertive Big Dog victories are that "been there, done that" power source. We draw on our positive experiences to build our self-belief.

Check out the additional examples of powerful *Big Dog Victories* on page 85, and there are many others that go all the way back to when we were little kids. We have hundreds, if not thousands of push-through-apprehension-and-go-for-it experiences. We just need to be mentally active and become skilled at recognizing when we break free of apprehension and execute, and when we do we tip our memory scale positive.

Now let's build our Big Dog highlight reel.

Building Our Highlight Reel

Pause and take a close look at the steps and the scenes in the *Replace* illustration on pages 92 and 93. Those two steps are a repeatable process to vividly remember when we kick apprehension's butt and go for it. The more details that we can remember and hold clear in our mind, the more power our Big Dog memories provide under pressure. In other words, we're going to build (and constantly update) our personal Big Dog highlight reel.

• *Point: replacing doubt with past success requires all of our Big Dog victories to be quickly and easily accessible.*

For example, where do you put our favorite shirts? Tucked away in the back of our closet or up front so they're easy to find? It's the same with our push-through-the-nerves experiences—we must keep them up front and center in our mind.

As we walk through the two Replace steps, Recall and Save/Play, we try to relive our competitive experiences with as much detail as possible. We relive the feelings and the emotions associate with each experience we're remembering, either from our sports life or our everyday life.

Step 1, Recall:

If you don't have video of competitive performances to watch and evaluate, do your best to remember specific experiences. We're going to recall two totally opposite competitive states: one when our overly emotional, doubter right brain was in control and we were apprehensive and doubtful, and the other when our levelheaded, believer left brain was in control and we were mentally tough and went for it.

First, let's analyze a crash-and-burn experience.

Perspective shift: It's important to start seeing negative experiences from a more mature perspective, as highly educational and motivating, not painful or demoralizing. This isn't some kind of Jedi mind trick. When we think objectively and evaluate the difficulties we have with apprehension, we then are able to conquer that feeling and turn the nervous energy into an advantage.

Back to crashing and burning: Which past experience comes to mind? Picture some of the details. Look your apprehensive reaction straight in the eyes. What overwhelmed you? Typically, apprehension is associated with feeling inferior. We don't feel we're up to the challenge; we don't feel we're good enough. Our embarrassment prevention software kicks in, adrenaline skyrockets, the Doubt Demons attack, then we puke, and if we don't take charge mentally, we look like we've never trained or played volleyball before. Here's the weirdest part: we repeat the same old, ineffective, worn-out approach game after game and tournament after tournament, which doesn't make sense.

As we're evaluating, we're not looking for flawed technique or physical mistakes. We're observing our apprehensive right brain in action, the part of us that lacks mental toughness and always hesitates. We ask ourselves the following questions: Why was I so apprehensive? Why was I distracted? Why did I hesitate? Which of the Doubt Demons were clouding my mind: Inadequacy, Past Failure, or Embarrassment? What was so intimidating?

 **"Courage is not the absence of fear, but the ability to carry on inspite of it."**

Mark Twain

1 RECALL
Appreciate your Big Dog victories.

❯ REPLACE

Crush apprehension by drawing self-belief from your past Big Dog success. Be mentally active and recall your "been there, done that" experiences,

We must objectively view those shaking-in-our-shoes moments, so we can clearly compare them to our Big Dog experiences. Make sure to name that specific crash and burn experience. Use the name of the school the match was played at, or an opponent's name, or "something." Just name the experience, so you can easily recall it under pressure.

2 SAVE/PLAY
Draw on your Big Dog success to crush doubt.

© 2012 Let's Win!

Next, we're going to watch or recall a totally opposite performance, a performance when we sucked it up and executed, despite the nerves. We ask ourselves (and answer) the following questions: Why wasn't I intimidated? Why was I mentally tough? How did I overcome the nerves? Answering, "I don't know," is mentally lazy. We must be mentally active and get to the bottom of *why* we were able to deal with the apprehension. That's where the "been there, done that" power comes from—in the *why*.

Vividly remember as many positive experiences as you can. Name each one as you stack them on top of each other. Try to identify what made the difference. Try to dissect why you were mentally tough and were able to push through the apprehension and execute. The more vivid the details, the clearer and more usable each memory experience becomes, providing more power and greater believability under pressure, which is what we're after.

Now let's move on to Step 2.

Step 2, Save/Play:

Once we've remembered and named our top Big Dog victories of all time, we must formally save them. This is the fantasy part of the process, but don't dismiss it. Be sure you understand this "mental storage device" idea. As we create mental pictures of our powerful Big Dog victories, we need to save them just like we'd store files on a computer, food in the fridge, or clothes in the closet.

This save/play task is to figure out what kind of mental storage device makes the most sense to you. Some of us skip the fantasy and keep a real notebook, like a positive Big Dog Victory Journal. Others may think of a mental flash drive, while others may think of burning a mental DVD. Personally, I have an imaginary oak filing cabinet with two drawers and each experience has its own folder.

It doesn't really matter which mental storage device we choose, the result we're after is to save all of our Big Dog success in the front of our mind to easily shift our thinking to when needed. We don't want to get caught searching our memories for reasons *why* we can believe when the competition and the Doubt Demons are banging down our door.

Are you seeing how this works? Quickly accessible past success stimulates the "been there, done that" response, which engages the levelheaded side of our brain. Then, rather than allowing our primal reactions to stop us in our tracks, we're able to offer a competent counterargument to that moment's apprehensive feeling.

Our self-belief is completely based on whether we believe in ourselves. Our self-belief is heavily influenced by what we remember most, either positive or negative experiences. And building our Big Dog highlight real is how we influence what we remember. Once we master the recall, save/play process, all of our positive experiences will be easily accessible. Then we're able to coach ourselves up, draw on success, and handle the heat.

Draw on Success

When the adrenaline hits and the Doubt Demons swarm reminding us of our weaknesses, past failures, and potential embarrassments, along with running a highlight video of our opponent's strengths, we must respond with a level head. We must forcefully shift our thinking from "what might go wrong" to the vivid memories of our "been there, done that" Big Dog success.

Think pink elephants. This has to be one of the best "shifting" stories I've heard in a long time. Let me explain. During the 2012 Olympic track and field trials, A. G. Kruger, a world-class hammer thrower was asked during an interview, "How do you handle the pressure?" Chuckling, this burly, 280 lb. Olympic hopeful hammer thrower says, "This may sound pretty weird, but I think of pink elephants." The interviewer looked puzzled, then A. G. lets out a hearty laugh and adds, "What I mean is, pink elephants are **We tell ourselves factual reasons why we can make the play and get the win.** so ridiculous, so absolutely unreal that it breaks the tension, it makes me laugh, it eases my mind so I can get back to thinking about what's important, throwing the hammer."

• *Point: come up with your own version of pink elephants to insert humor into intensely nervy situations, so you can easily shift your thinking from apprehension to fierceness by drawing on all your Big Dog success.*

Breaking a severe meltdown cycle might require briefly shifting our focus to things we value and appreciate outside of sports: family, friends, a significant other, our education, our job, music, hobbies, the list goes on. It helps put the drama in perspective. *"Yeah, it's high-stakes, but it's not a life-or-death situation."* We force ourselves to face the nerves, breathe, and then coach ourselves up. We give ourselves an adult pep talk and tell ourselves factual reasons *why* we can make the play and get the win.

That's not repeating "positive" statements (PMA). It's much more. Talking to ourselves about *why* we can is not just saying to ourselves, "I can, I can, I can." *Why* we can is purposefully narrowing our self-talk to our solid counterarguments, which are based on our actual experiences. It's solid strategy, not flighty emotion. When we shift our thinking to justthe upcoming match or next serve, our solid mechanics, and then pumping up our core self-belief, we get it done.

• *Point: we must become an excellent arguer with ourselves.*

Envision the process of drawing on success as a sequence of mental toughness skills, we (1) anticipate our primal fears before reaching the meltdown point, (2) make sure we've switched to our fierce Big Dog attacker or protector attitude, (3) kick in some competitive breathing and toughen up, (4) narrow our focus to just SMS and the 3 Battle Zones, and (5) *replace* apprehension with our own believable "been there, done that" Big dog success. That's how we coach ourselves up. We talk to ourselves, we don't listen to ourselves. We picture what we want. We stay checked in mentally, constantly breathing (deeply), and telling ourselves *why* we've got this and *why* we're going to get it done.

As we're building our Big Dog highlight reel, we must be patient! When our mind wanders, we just relax and bring it back on track. It's similar to being in class and realizing we've been drifting off and haven't heard a word, and click, we tune right back in. A similar example of a wandering mind is reading a page but not retaining much, so we go back and reread the page. But a wandering mind in competition is devastating—we don't get do-overs. When our mind wanders, we force ourselves to narrow our focus and concentrate. That's how we win.

As we close this chapter realize that (1) all of us are much braver and grittier competitors than we give ourselves credit for, (2) we all have a ton of success, if we just pay attention, and (3) we already have "it." Rehearse (visualize) letting your Big Dog out, crushing apprehension, and going for it. See yourself stepping into the spotlight, letting the crowd stare, 100% believing, and pulling the trigger.

Now you know how to *replace doubt*—with all of your "been there, done that" Big Dog success.

CRUSH DOUBT

5 REPLACE

Don't let apprehension get out of control. Attack!
Use your Big Dog success to knock out doubt.

TOURNAMENT PROCESS

Keep your memory scale weighted positively.

FOCUS POINT

Put your Big Dog highlight reel on autoplay—all day.

THE BIG 3

SELF-TALK

"I've nailed it before, so I can nail it again."

VISUALIZE

Picture memories of succeeding. Draw on the power.

ADAPT

Coach yourself up. Believe 100% and go for it!

WinningSTATE
The Mental Toughness Company

6 BELIEVE
WIN THE BATTLE

How deeply do you believe, in yourself? How authentic
is your conviction? How well do you concentrate?
WinningSTATE athletes skillfully concentrate on "focus
points" to believe in themselves 100% rather than fall
victim to uncontested apprehension and doubt.

Win the battle! Become skilled at believing instead of doubting.
If we don't *BELIEVE* 100%, how can we expect to handle the
nerves, fiercely complete, and win? We can't, unless we're relying on luck.
WinningSTATE athletes possess a mental game to get out of their own way
and accomplish their dream.

Mental toughness under pressure, simply put, comes down to concentration. We're either consumed by distractions and apprehension or we're
mentally tough, 100% focused on executing.

Professional golfer and on-air analyst Paul Azinger put it well when he
said, "Concentration is not a gift. It doesn't come naturally. Concentration
is a learned behavior. It's an art form. It's beautiful to watch."

We agree. The elusive aspect of battlefield concentration is not confidence, it's lacking points to concentrate on, which is the learned behavior
part of Azinger's statement. Consider this: How can we expect ourselves
to concentrate under pressure if we don't have anything to concentrate on?
We can't. Our tournament process must include specific focus points or the
Doubt Demons have their way.

"Be a mental game giant. Build focus points that anchor your self-belief."

Our switch ritual, SMS, the 3 Battle Zones, pre-planned fueling, know-ing our primal competitive reaction, breathing, rehearsing, and having our Big Dog victories easily accessible are all focus points we use as mental weapons to take out apprehension and execute with Big Dog crush-the-competition conviction. Pre-programming our *focus points* is how we stop flip-flopping around from doubting to believing and back to doubting. We pin our mental activity to focus points that anchor our self-belief.

• *Point: we take charge of our apprehensive reactions by concentrating on specific focus points.*

Stop Flip-Flopping

The following true story demonstrates that believing in ourselves, or not believing in ourselves, is all in our head.

A few years back I traveled with a local high school wrestling team to the Reno Tournament of Champions—a huge national tournament. Reaching the podium in Reno meant All-American status. I was sort of the team mom. I shuttled the team back and forth from the hotel, kept the tournament fuel flowing, and helped the coaches and wrestlers with whatever they needed.

One of our middleweights made it to the medal rounds and was wres-tling for third/fourth. I'll call him "our guy." I was chilling in the stands, and awhile before his match our guy came up and asked if I'd seen the coaches. He didn't look good, sort of clammy and grayish. I thought to my-self, "Oh man, he's melting down." I didn't know where the coaches were, and he spun around and took off.

Minutes later he was back, this time having problems with a kneepad. The problem wasn't significant, but when we're melting down, everything is catastrophic. In the middle of telling me about the kneepad issue, he turned and took off. He was coming unglued.

I went and found the coaches on the arena floor and told them that our guy was falling apart. Right about then our guy found us and told the coaches about the kneepad problem. One of the coaches went off to find him a backup. One of the other coaches slapped him on the shoulder and said, "You'll be fine," and that was going to be the end of it. This kid was ready to throw up.

Respectfully, I told the Head Coach (who is an awesome man) that our guy needed to be talked down and got the green light to work with him. I asked our guy to go for a walk, and as we got to the other end of the arena I asked him, "Do you like homework?"

He looked at me and could barely get out the answer, "No, not really."

"Got a girlfriend?"

"Yeah."

"You like to go fishing?"

"What?" he asked, with a totally confused stare.

"What about cars? You like cars?" The random real-world questions were confusing him; he was expecting a stereotypical pep talk, but as we talked about absolutely nothing, reality started creeping back in. The random real-world questions were disengaging his nerves. It's fascinating to watch someone's mind come back from a meltdown.

Once I started to see his eyes clear and his mind calm down, I asked why his opponent was in his kitchen. He grinned and without hesitating said, "Because yesterday he beat me in the semis." And with that statement our guy saw his fear and was then able to be real with himself. Keep in mind, whoever won the upcoming match would receive All-American status—it was a BIG deal.

"So basically, you can't win," I said.

"No, I can win," he snapped right back.

"How?" I asked with a "whatever" kind of a tone. Our guy stared right at me and rattled off his opponent's weaknesses and his strengths, and then out loud, move by move, relived the entire match from the day before. At the end of his description, he was amused with himself at why he was so shaken up.

THE 3 DOUBT DEMONS

The 3 Doubt Demons are constantly lurking. They make us feel small, weak, and not worthy. Guess what? We don't have to listen. We can come to our own defense.

EMBARRASSMENT
Makes us think we're being laughed at.

INADEQUACY
Makes us feel weak and inferior.

PAST FAILURE
Reminds us of poor performances.

JENNY'S FEARS

SPOTLIGHT FLOATER TITLE MATCH

"I can beat this kid," he said with conviction.

I laughed, punched him on the shoulder, and said, "Exactly." We went back over those thoughts and mental images several times, and I told our guy he needed to stay right where he was mentally, focused on his strengths and his opponent's weaknesses.

• *Point: our guy had a "factual" conversation with himself, the opposite of emotionally fluffy nonsense.*

A few minutes later our guy was back on earth and looking forward to kicking some butt. He was in a solid space emotionally and had a totally different look and feel. Our guy wrestled a dominant match, pinning his archrival in the third period. It was very exciting to watch. Our guy's an All-American for life.

The story continues.

Those two rivals met again twice at other tournaments before State. Our guy beat his archrival soundly both times; our guy owned him, or so it seemed. At State our guy was ranked number 1 and the other guy was ranked number 2. The rankings played out and they were in the finals. This was going to be an awesome match to watch; we all anticipated, of course, that our guy would emerge a State Champion.

I wasn't in the trenches with the team at State, so I watched from the stands. As the match began I knew within seconds our guy was twisted; he opened tentative and was on his heels. The other guy was tentative as well, having been beaten three times in the previous two months, but once he realized that our guy was apprehensive, he gained a huge amount of power and turned it on. If you know what you're looking for, you can see it on video.

In the second period, probably from being full of doubt and hesitating, our guy rolled his ankle. He did his best to recover, but his archrival hung on and defended well in the third to become State Champion. What a year! Our guy owned his opponent, but he let him back in mentally at the State tournament because of apprehension and doubt. And the doubt was pure fantasy, since he had beaten his rival three times previously under tremendous pressure.

We have all seen or lived a story like this and it's so important to realize…it's all in our head.

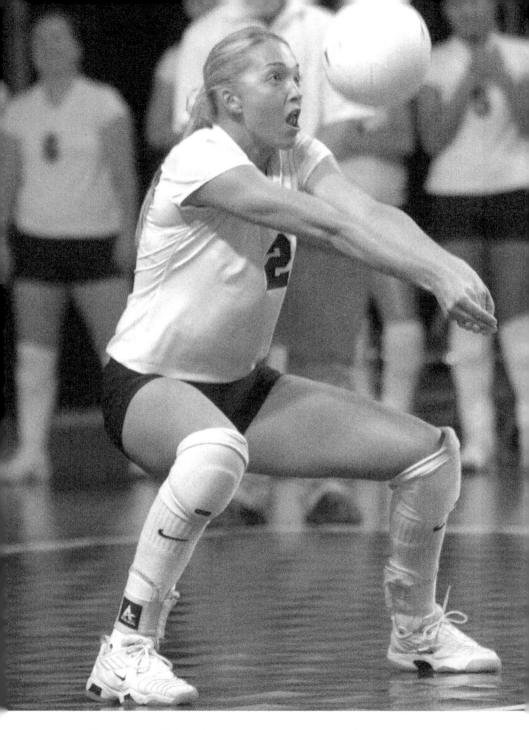

Winona State University senior setter Katie Matel in a solid position both physically and mentally. Photo by *Staff/www. winonastatewarriors.com*

"Everyone's watching..."

"I can't!"

"AAHHH!!!"

LITTLE DOG **REACTIONS**

BELIEVE

Take charge of your mental state. Give yourself a pep talk. Use your mental jiu-jitsu. Crush apprehension! Narrow your focus and force yourself to believe!

• *Point: we must aggressively build focus points to crush doubt, believe 100%, and fiercely compete.*

Self-Talk (Work Your Mental Jiu-Jitsu)

Telling ourselves not to think about negative thoughts or to not hesitate or to not do "anything" is not an action. How can we aspire to not do something? We can't. We must have prepared focus points we shift our thinking to that are positive actions. Instead of hearing ourselves say, "I can't do

BIG DOG **RESPONSES**

this and I can't do that," we tell ourselves, "I'm going to do this, and here's why!" This mental shift takes practice to be smooth and automatic—it's sort of like mental jiu-jitsu. When our nerves flare, we must be able to put our doubter right brain in a choke hold and tap the dream¬¬¬-crusher out. We do that by being mentally active and engaging in aggressive, drill-sergeant-like self-talk.

Are you seeing how handling the nerves by coaching ourselves up works? The trick to jumpstarting our levelheaded response to surging nerves is asking ourselves *questions*. First, we anticipate the nerves and take a breath, then we start the self-talk discussion, which is much more than PMA. A *WinningSTATE* athlete's self-talk is drill sergeant like; it's pointed, direct, aggressive, in-your-face. It's grounded in facts, not hopes or flighty wishful thinking. It goes something like: "What the heck is going on? Get a grip! Of course I'm freaking out. Don't be ridiculous. Breathe. Concentrate. I'm focusing on executing. I'm gonna step up and kill it. Watch this!"

Since this book is G-Rated, I must refrain from providing a more graphic version of a veteran competitor's self-talk. We have a tendency to smack ourselves around when the nerves are getting out of control.

Get the point? Feel the edge? Forcefully engaging our self-talk with intelligent questions, instead of emotionally pleading to be saved, quickly makes our levelheaded, mentally tough, doubt-free voice the dominant voice in our head. We must be our own drill sergeant. We de-dramatize the nerves by focusing our self-talk on facts and past success. I cannot stress enough the importance of *forcing* rational, levelheaded thoughts during emotionally challenging situations. We must step back, take a breath, and ride the adrenaline. We must use the apprehension, not allow it to drag us around all over the place. That's what separates champions from the rest of the pack: commanding mental toughness that controls the nerves and fuels self-belief. Champions don't fold under pressure.

• *Point: focusing on real-world questions is how we take our apprehensive Little Dog by the neck, firmly sit it down, concentrate, and let our Big Dog out.*

Take this to heart: Before and during competition our mind is always hyperactive. We never stop assessing the failure-potential of a high-pressure situation. Ever! We must take charge of our mental state and coach ourselves up by forcefully responding to nerves with aggressive self-talk and positive mental pictures.

VISUALIZE (Play Your Big Dog Highlight Reel)

I'm sure it's becoming clear that handling apprehension and distraction under any amount of pressure comes down to what's going on in our head. Are our self-talk and mental pictures positive or negative? Are the nerves in control or are we in control? Are we focused on "never giving up" or on "I'm going to win this"? Never giving up is expected. Never giving up is a prerequisite to being a fearsome competitor. Of course there are a hundred reasons to give up, to let out that big "I'm done" breath. But pushing through our quitter reaction and not being broken is not mental toughness, that's not being a pansy. We must also be smart and calculating, along with fiercely determined. We must keep a clear head, along with never giving up.

Take a look at the *Believe* illustration above, the battle over doubting vs. believing. That's the real battle, right? That's not the never-give-up battle or the confidence battle. That's the self-belief battle. Ask yourself which brain wins the battle in your head? How deeply do you believe in yourself? When apprehension looms large, what are your mental jiu-jitsu countermoves? What do you visualize? Our mental pictures are just as important as our crunch-time self-talk.

Learn to draw power and conviction from visualizing your past Big Dog success. Smile inside!

For example: I've interviewed numerous state champions across all sports, and a D1 soccer player, a striker (scorer), put it best when I asked, "What do you think about before a big game or a big play?"

"That's easy," he replied, "I think about all of the times I've scored, in detail."

The tone and conviction in his voice was the telling part; it was clear, forceful, and believable. Those memories of success were part of his Big Dog highlight reel, and they provided him with deep, unflinching self-belief and conviction.

• *Point: Point: build and update your Big Dog highlight real.*

Picture it. We're nervous with expectation, our hands are trembling, our mouth is full of cotton, and our foot is vibrating so fast it's a blur, but then we see ourselves shifting our thinking to visualizing our Big Dog victories. We also hear our factual, drill-sergeant-like self-talk. The nervousness changes. It decreases, doesn't it? Then, once we put a crack in apprehension's armor, we continue the counterattack with more mental jiu-jitsu: we press the aggressive self-talk and visualizing more Big Dog success. The goal is actually doing it under the gun—that's being mentally tough when it counts.

Even though Chapter 5 drove this point home, we must clearly know our top Big Dog victories of all time, so ask yourself how many times have you relived each of them, play by play? Do you play 'em on your personal YouTube channel? They should have several hundred plays each. Be your own TV commentator. Learn to draw power and conviction from visualizing your past Big Dog success. Smile inside!

Practice, practice, practice. Or to put it in a mental game way: rehearse, rehearse, rehearse. Turn your Big Dog victories over and over and over in your mind. Be able to describe them in vivid detail. Be able to easily access all of your Big Dog success when it counts.

Now let's walk through a tournament process to bring all of the skills and routines together for the competition.

ADAPT (Work Your Tournament Process)

Performing well under pressure requires overcoming constant, in-our-face adversity and letting go of any mistakes. Performing well is not just about getting knocked down and immediately getting back up, no hesitation, it's also about skillfully dealing with our nervy primal reactions to the public spotlight. In other words, do we fight, flee, or freeze, and to what degree? The majority of SEAL recruits fail water competency the first time. Those who pass in the remaining attempts face their "I'm gonna die" response head-on and engage in levelheaded self-talk. They forcefully think their way through the nerves, rather than emotionally panicking and melting down.

Tournaments are full of similar, yet not as intense, primal survival reactions, starting with the evening before and going all the way through to stepping onto the court. Pause and take a look at the *Tournament Process* illustrations on the following pages. In Chapter 2 we highlighted three physical locations, the battle zones, to reduce the size of the arena and eliminate distractions. Now we need to add two more battle zones to our tournament process: the evening before and the morning of a tournament. Some would argue that these two time periods, the evening before and the morning of a tournament, are when many of us get overwhelmed with nervous expectations and never recover. In other words, the evening before and the morning of really are battle zones.

The Evening Before:

Typically, practice is light the day (or two) before a tournament. Since we're in great shape and excited to compete, we're full of energy…but there's nothing to do. That's why the evening before is a mental battle zone. The evening before a tournament we have one job and one job only: to relax!

East Carolina University middle hitter Kelly Derby (4) takes a swing against University of Central Florida's Kristin Fisher (7). Photo by *Replay Photos/ www.flickr.com/carolinarob7*

The evening before is all about limiting distractions, relaxing, and getting a good night's rest. This can be a difficult task when the stakes are high, the competition is stacked, and we want to perform our best. From moment to moment our minds race and our nerves surge. Combine this with restlessness and outside social distractions, and the evening before can be a serious energy drain if we don't have a plan.

Yes, I've heard stories about athletes from back in the day who could party all night and set world records the next day. Those one in a billion phenoms might have been able to pull that off during the pre-modern sports era, but most of today's sports are so stacked and so deep it requires world-class concentration on and off the court to compete successfully at a high level.

• *Point: the majority of us must focus on competing and skip the socializing.*

We start our tournament process the evening before. We restrict our activities and what's going on in our head. We do our best to let go of all the competitive expectations. We want to store up the Superwoman juice, so we must chill out and quiet our emotional right brain down.

We must be careful when checking in with friends over the phone. We don't want to get involved in a bunch of questions non-competitors have a tendency to ask, like "how do you think you're gonna do?" or "aren't you nervous?" The match will come soon enough. We must stay in the present, which is doing absolutely nothing but relaxing and resting.

Here's a reality check: we can't get any stronger, faster, or quicker twenty-four hours before a match. The physical preparation is done. Our job the evening before is to physically rest and mentally rehearse our tournament process.

Picture a giant Jumbotron (which is a form of visualizing) and the following scrolling message: SETTLE DOWN! CONTROL YOUR THOUGHT PROCESS. We must force our mind to do what we want it to do. We start that process the evening before; it's sort of a practice session. When our nerves are noisy, or when our energy is high and we'd rather be running around "doing stuff," we control our thought process and our activities by

Chill Out & Relax

Start your "tournament process." Conserve energy, don't expend it.

Plan Some Activities

Read, watch a movie, play a video game, whatever, just relax.

Get Horizontal

Don't worry about "deep" sleep; just lie down with lights out/cell phones off.

TOURNAMENT PROCESS
THE EVENING BEFORE

The evening before a tournament we have one job and one job only: to relax! The evening before we want to limit distractions, relax, and get a good night's "rest."

using our mental jiu-jitsu to take control, calm ourselves down, stay in the moment, and relax. We accomplish that by shifting our thinking, giving ourselves an inspiring self-talk, and then doing what we would normally do to relax: read, watch movies, play video games, draw, knit, whatever.

• *Point: we conserve energy, we don't expend it.*

We must be in command, not our primal nervous energy. Tournament behavior starts the evening before. For the big tournaments, it starts several nights before. The primary objective is getting (and staying) horizontal! Our bodies rest best when lying down, so we make sure we're lying down and chilling out for the evening. Despite the high energy, we must control our activities and stay planted on the couch or on the bed. If falling asleep for

THE MORNING OF

Fuel & Organize

Fuel up, organize your stuff. There's nothing to do, so chill out!

Rehearse

Review SMS and your job at each battle zone. Play your highlight reel.

Welcome the Butterflies

Don't resist, get the butterflies to fly in formation.

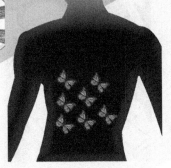

TOURNAMENT PROCESS
THE MORNING OF

The morning of a tournament is similar to the evening before. We chill out! We fuel well, organize our stuff, and store up the Superwoman juice for the match.

the night is tough, don't worry about it. "Deep sleep" is not the goal. As long as we're lying down with lights out and cell phones off, we'll wake up rested and ready to kick some butt.

• *Point: we get horizontal, we stay horizontal, and we chill out!*

The Morning Of:

You know what wins matches, right? One swing, which means there's nothing to do until the first swing. The morning of a tournament is similar to the evening before. We stay in chill mode! There's nothing to do but fuel well, organize our stuff, and get to the arena, so mentally and emotionally we chill out and conserve our energy. We trick ourselves into disengaging from the expectations by talking to ourselves—out loud if necessary. We must give our mind something positive to do. We make sure our levelheaded,

THE STANDS/BENCH

Rest, Fuel & Hydrate

Fresh fruit, PB&J, bagel and cream cheese, nut mix, and lots of H$_2$O.

Mentally Check In

Say goodbye to friends & family. Put on some music and go to sleep.

Crush Apprehension

Grab the Doubt Demons by the neck and shut 'em up. Be mentally active.

TOURNAMENT PROCESS
THE STANDS/BENCH

The stands/bench are not only where we rest, fuel, hydrate, and rehearse focus points, we also make sure our fierce, competitive Big Dog is in control, not our social self.

believer left brain is in control. Our doubter right brain will be babbling all kinds of unstable "what if this?" and "what if that?" about things that may or may not happen. All of that "what if?" stuff is nothing but an apprehensive, nerves-induced, emotional energy drain—and it's completely counterproductive. We keep our thoughts and feelings focused in the present and on the positive. We stay completely away from any negative "what if something goes wrong?" hypothetical scenarios. Of course something could go wrong. It's more productive to focus on what might go right.

When we wander into thinking about the tournament, we simply shift our thinking to doing some planning. We organize our tournament process in our head. We see ourselves arriving at the venue with our sports bag full of everything we need.

Switch Attitudes

Light your competitive fire. Attacker or protector, fight back!

Love the Nerves

Nerves are a good thing. Think your way though the moment.

Ride the Adrenaline

Use the Superwoman juice. Focus on your Big Dog highlight reel.

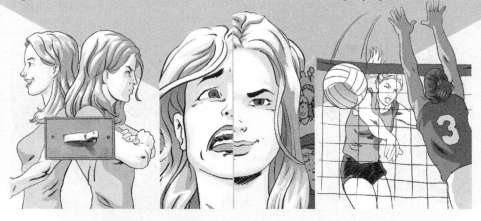

TOURNAMENT PROCESS
THE COURT

Nothing exists outside of the court. Absolutely nothing! What's job #1 on the court? Crushing apprehension. We mentally take charge, get fierce, and concentrate on SMS.

Next, we connect with our job between matches; we see ourselves resting and fueling, not running around playing social "I forgot why I was here" games. We're there to compete, not mess around. Multi-match tournaments require frequent resting, fueling, and hydrating, so the morning of we make sure we're prepared to get the fueling/hydrating job done. This rest and fuel break strategy is important, because so few volleyball players put resting and fueling breaks in their tournament process. Planning when to turn our laser-beam focus off to allow our decision-making machine to cool down is just as important as planning when to turn it on. It's impossible to stay intensely focused for an entire tournament, so planning when to take brief rest and fuel breaks is not only smart, it's essential to winning. Make resting and fueling a priority.

Breathe Deeply

You are in control, not the nerves. Get lots of air. Breathe!

Focus on SMS

Forcefully narrow your focus to the situation, mechanics, and success.

You Already Have "It"

Believe! Free yourself of doubt by concentrating on your focus points.

TOURNAMENT PROCESS

THE SERVICE AREA

As we step up to the line we gotta be breathing big and believing big. We gotta be ready to win the battle. We crush doubt by focusing on The Big 3 and SMS.

Before leaving for the arena the morning of a tournament, there's nothing we can do to improve our chances of success other than controlling the nerves, resting, and going over our tournament process and our focus points. So we chill out and talk to ourselves about believing. We don't need to increase our confidence, we just need to not doubt. We pop in a favorite movie, listen to some music, or read a book, and breathe.

• *Point: we organize our stuff, fuel up, stay positive by visualizing our Big Dog highlight reel, and chill out.*

The Stands (The Bench):

Once we enter the arena, where's the first place we go (other than the restroom)? To the stands or the bench. We set up command central. The stands

BELIEVE in your heart, your mechanics, and your past Big Dog success.

are not only where we rest, fuel, hydrate, and rehearse focus points, the stands and the bench are also where we make sure our fierce, competitive Big Dog is in control, not our social self. Of course we say hi, acknowledge people, shake hands, and smile. But inside we're reserved and focused. That doesn't mean we're mean mugging life. Of course we're lighthearted, humorous, and fun. But we don't get lost in the event or the commotion. Our core attitude is deliberate, we know why we're there: we're there to fiercely compete.

As we react to the largeness of the battleground environment and seeing other competitors, the butterflies can easily swell to gut-tightening apprehension. What do we do? *We respond.* We don't just react. We think. We get the butterflies to fly in formation. We talk ourselves through the moment, "Alright, here we are. Dang. I am nervous." We coach ourselves up. "Let's get a grip. We need to shift our thinking and plug into SMS." If we're not nervous, then cool, we stay in chill mode and do our job in the stands, which is to rest, fuel, and rehearse. We conserve energy, we don't expend it.

At multi-match tournaments as time counts down to our first or next match, our nerves will always flare, so we don't passively sit in the stands hoping everything will somehow work out for the best. We mentally take charge by being our own drill sergeant. We restrict our concentration to our main focus points: (1) our Big Dog Highlight real, and (2) our switch ritual. We talk to ourselves in our own version of drill-sergeant fierceness, and we visualize our favorite Big Dog victories over and over and over. We use the time in the stands wisely to crush apprehension and boost our self-belief. We stay mentally active and don't get caught up in any negativity. The only thing that matters in the stands is forcefully getting our mind right for the next match. So we check our Grr Factor, fuel up to keep our competitive fire blazing, and we make it clear to ourselves that we're going to fiercely compete and take home the win.

Sleep clarification: it's ok if we're a little groggy and foggy-headed after waking up. That means we did a good job, we actually fell asleep. Don't worry, we wake up fast, especially once it's time to get ready for the next match and the adrenaline starts flowing. We'll be wide awake and fully recharged.

• *Point: we come back to command central after every match and fuel up, rest, and mentally grab the positive. We get horizontal!*

The Court:

As we step out to the court, self-consciousness really kicks in and our primal emotions surge—we can feel them in our chest. If it's a multi-match tournament, the commotion is extreme. This is why prepared focus points are a necessity. We must restrict our concentration to our job. Nothing exists except the court. Absolutely nothing! What's job #1 on the court? Crushing apprehension. How do we do that? We mentally take charge and concentrate on SMS. What crowd? What title? What doubt? Who cares who's watching and what they're thinking. We shift our focus from all of that external self-consciousness, ego stuff to internal competitive SMS. That's it!

Keeping our head right during a set is tactical. Sometimes we have the momentum and "feel" dominant, yet other times we don't. We must be smart. Early in the match we don't want to exhaust ourselves, we want to conserve the Superwoman juice. Completing mentally tough is not being all tense, holding our breath, or mean mugging other competitors. That's not handling the nerves. That's the opposite. That's posturing and letting our primal reactions dictate our behavior. We keep our head right by responding, breathing, and talking ourselves down, "Hey! Bring it down a notch (or three)." Countless athletes consume way too much energy early in the match.

On the court, distractions can be difficult, and handling distractions is not one size fits all. Some of us handle distractions more easily than others. For example: some people read effectively in a crowded, noisy room. For

"Whether you think you can or you can't you're probably right."
Henry Ford

me that's impossible. I'm easily distracted, especially by noise. For me, tournament environments are very chaotic, so I tend to get focused and somewhat selfish right from the start. Unlike some competitors, who can flip the switch and be in battle mode in an instant, for me switching attitudes takes more concentration. In other words, I've got to climb into my fiercely competitive Big Dog protector "you gotta go through me" attitude—the paint your face, sharpen your weapon kind of ritual we spoke of in Chapter 1. What about you? Can you quickly and easily switch attitudes or does it take a bit longer to let your Big Dog out and be a wrecking ball of a competitor?

• *Point: make your switch ritual a priority.*

On the court, the Doubt Demons are bent on convincing us we're not good enough, but we still have time to grab them by the neck and convince them why they're wrong. We shoot down their hater nonsense with our rehearsed, realistic, inspiring self-talk. We breathe and concentrate on SMS as we give ourselves an adult pep-talk.

• *Point: we must be our own best friend. We must coach ourselves up.*

Warming up, we're moments away from stepping into the batter's box, and most of the time it will produce an intense adrenaline rush. Let's pause briefly and talk more about adrenaline. Adrenaline's bottom line is RUN! When we feel threatened, glands dump adrenaline into our bloodstream, which quickly increases our physical and mental capabilities. This is obviously a good thing. But on the court we must remain calm, which is really tough when the Superwoman juice is pouring into our bloodstream telling us to sprint around the venue or go climb up the wall.

If the Doubt Demons are winning the internal battle, adrenaline can cause all sorts of negative side effects: we feel lightheaded, sometimes nauseated (yep, some puke), and unfocused. Poorly handled adrenaline does the opposite of what it's intended to do; it extinguishes our competitive fire, leaving us feeling lethargic and tired—sort of a letdown. However, when we manage the adrenaline with breathing and concentrating on SMS, we feel like Superwoman, ready to leap tall buildings and fiercely compete. If we were strapped with a heart-rate indicator and a blood-pressure monitor

Wood River High Schools' middle hitter Morgan Fischer gets some serious air at the Lou-Platte Confrence Tournament. Photo by *HMFRphotos/ www.flickr.com/hmfrphotos*

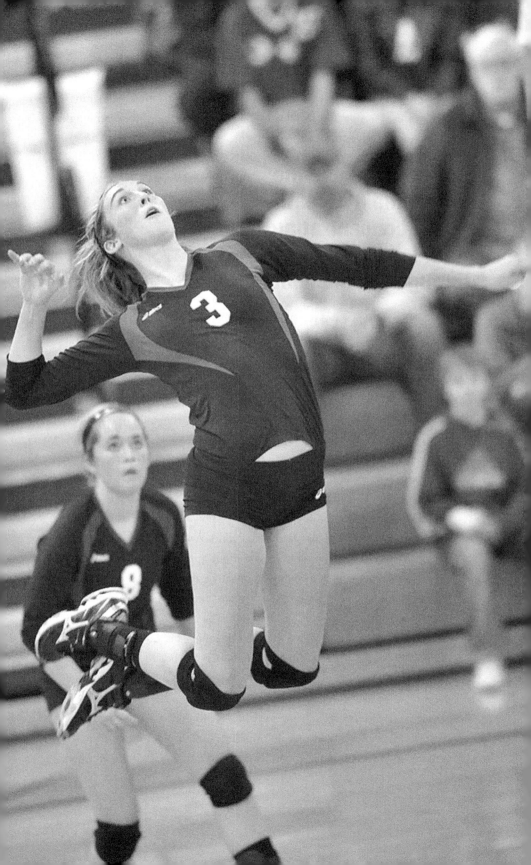

during an adrenaline rush, we'd be amazed. Our heart is pounding and our blood pressure is soaring every time. We must control it, rather than letting it control us. We ride and use the adrenaline by breathing, concentrating, and talking ourselves through the moment.

We ride and use the adrenaline by breathing, concentrating, and talking our self through the moment.

• *Point: we smile inside, talk ourselves through the adrenaline rush, and have some fun. Yes, have some fun!*

We can count on the Doubt Demons always being in our ear play after play, at both ends of the court. So as we go through our stretching and warm-up routine, we visualize our Big Dog victories and focus our self-talk on "why" we can believe. We crush doubt and stay in the flow of the set.

The Service Area:

As we step up to the line our emotions surge, our heart rate and breathing increase. Even though mentally everything is happening at an incredibly fast pace, it is vital to have the presence of mind to know where we are on the Grr Meter. If we're emotionally tweaked, or overly angry, we need to coach ourselves up and get in our grove.

This is why PMA and visualizing victory aren't very effective. Saying to ourselves, "I can, I can, I can," isn't very powerful if our core doesn't believe it. It's emotional, not factual. Of course we want it and of course we can. Visualizing victory is worthless if our apprehensive right brain is in control and our core is dwelling on negative, future obsessing "what if" scenarios. We let go of "what might happen" negativity, so we can make something happen.

As we're getting set, we've gotta be breathing big and believing big. BREATHE! Nerves tighten our gut and shorten our breath. Breathe in the stands, breathe on the bench, breathe on the court, and keep breathing all the way to the final point.

Think of competing as being very similar to giving a presentation in front of a group. We study the information well, but we don't visualize walking to the front of the room, turning around, and facing the crowd.

That's the shocker. When we turn around, look up, and see all of those faces and judgmental eyes staring straight at us. We study the information but don't visualize ourselves actually giving the presentation. Are you making the connection to serving? We train our technique, but we don't visualize competing in a match. We must study the information as well as rehearse giving the presentation.

Remember that we don't need to love the spotlight, but we must train ourselves to get comfortable with those nervy feelings of being center stage and being watched. Then we narrow our concentration to just SMS and believing. That's all we can do, ever.

- *Point: we gotta love the nerves, free ourselves of doubt, and go for it!*

The primary reason to build a tournament process that includes specific focus points is so we can get out of our own way and compete. So we can get fierce and let your Big Dog out. So we can climb into that killer instinct, that every-woman-for-herself mindset. We don't just throw the ball up; we get deliberate, dig in, and follow through. As we walk off the court we want coach saying, "Was that clutch or what? You were fearless. You did exactly what we talked about. You executed!"

Achieving a Winning State of Mind

As we close this chapter, I need to isolate one more term that is key to our success. A way of doing things that is vital to achieving a reliable winning state of mind: being deliberate.

Being deliberate in everything we do increases the potential for success no matter what we're doing. Being deliberate releases our passion in a focused way. Being deliberate is the absolute opposite of random, haphazard, disorganized or messy. Consider the synonyms for deliberate: purposeful, premeditated, intentional, calculated, planned, thoughtful, careful, measured, methodical, and the list goes on. For example, it took deliberate effort to learn to dig, block, pass, and swing. It will also take deliberate effort to plan your tournament process and to identify your focus points to use as your mental jiu-jitsu countermoves. This highly competitive sports culture we live in requires that we must be deliberate in everything we do.

- *Point: it takes deliberate, unflinching effort to believe in ourselves 100% when it's go-time.*

When we deliberately prepare positive responses to apprehensive reactions, the result is a solid, deep-down belief in ourselves. We call this a winning state of mind, and it's the holy grail of delivering clutch performances. This winning state is not a random event. It doesn't come from a supernatural force that blesses us on some days and not on others. A winning state of mind is achieved through world-class concentration that crushes apprehension, obliterates distractions, and genuinely pumps up our self-belief.

And most importantly, we must smile inside and have some fun. We must commit 100% to crushing our opponents. We must step into the batter's box filled to the brim with self-belief and conviction, not hyper-self-consciousness, apprehension, doubt, and hesitation.

Consider this: while others may believe in us, the only believing that matters is if we believe in ourselves, so we must skillfully get out of our own way and believe.

Now you know how to believe in yourself—and win the mental battle.

See you in the championship!

WIN THE BATTLE

6 BELIEVE

Be a mental game giant. Take charge and respond! Compete mentally tough and believe in yourself.

TOURNAMENT PROCESS

Plan your job. Mentally check in.

FOCUS POINT

Be deliberate. Crush doubt.

THE BIG 3

SELF-TALK

"I am mentally tough. Bring it!"

VISUALIZE

Picture thinking, believing, and executing.

ADAPT

Think your way through the nerves. Believe!

WinningSTATE
The Mental Toughness Company

7 DREAM
RISE ABOVE

What inspires you? What fills your heart with passion? Are you willing to work hard (and smart) to achieve success? *WinningSTATE* athletes have a dream so powerful it propels them past mediocrity and inspires them to work hard and excel.

E verything is possible. Become skilled at *dreaming* of big achievements.
     If we don't have a *DREAM* we're passionate about, we lack the drive to train hard and sacrifice while others socialize and hang out. *WinningSTATE* athletes accomplish outstanding achievements because their dream compels them to prevent anything from getting in their way to attain it.

Reality check: There's only one road to a state or national championship and it's called d-e-d-i-c-a-t-i-o-n. And Dedication Drive is paved with discipline, which is why so many great athletes come up short—lack of dedication and discipline is the champion destroyer.

Every day we're faced with decisions of whether to work or socialize. The cars, cash, contraband, social media, and *extreme socializing* (partying) are constant distractions that prevent personal achievement. I'm not preaching here; I'm cluing you in on how to win and what will drag you down. We must grasp the fact that a vivid, attainable dream is what drives success, any kind of success.

• *Point: We must foster a dream that gives us goosebumps. A dream we must achieve or "life just won't be right."*

"Passionately commit to achieving. Inspire your decisions with a life-changing dream."

If our desire is to become a champion, to distinguish ourselves from the average, to some degree we must separate ourselves from the majority of our peers who are more focused on fun and immediate gratification rather than work and future achievement. Our party peers who are uninspired individuals do not have a dream or any passion to accomplish something extraordinary. We do!

While writing *WinningSTATE—FOOTBALL*, I was communicating with Assistant Coach Blaine Davidson of the Bellevue High School Wolverines (Washington State), and at the bottom of his e-mails was the following quote.

> "The things that failures don't like to do are the very same things that you and I, including the successful, naturally like to do. We have to realize right from the start that success is something achieved by the minority, and is therefore unnatural and not to be achieved by following our natural likes and dislikes, nor by being guided by our natural preferences and prejudices."   —Albert Gray.

As that quote expresses so well, we won't see or meet very many people during our lifetime who are genuinely striving to excel and accomplish something extraordinary. Why? It's too scary. The majority of people lack the passion, the motivation, and the discipline to make courageous decisions. Decisions the average person won't make. How about you? Can you make extraordinary decisions? Or are you more concerned with what people think and how you fit in? Can you make decisions that make you different from most of the people around you? In America today, separating ourselves from our over-texting, over-indulging, over-socializing, dreamless party peers in order to train and excel is a courageous decision.

Don't you agree? Decisions that lead to accomplishing something big are motivated by having our sights on something we seriously want, something we're willing to work for, something that drives our decision- making to say, "no thanks," to being lazy or overly socializing and instead go physically train or mentally prepare. When there is no party to go to, there is no decision to make. That's easy. But when we have options to either train or hang out, *decisions must be made.*

Decisions that lead to accomplishing something big are motivated by having our sights on something we seriously want...

Realize that the majorities' natural tendencies are to play and have fun, not to work and achieve—let alone to work hard and excel. But to accomplish outstanding feats in the sports arena, we must discipline our natural tendencies by putting them in perspective and managing them. We just don't get in the game; we win the game—the mental game.

Black or White

This work-or-play decision is typically fought with extreme anxiety, but the outcome is black or white. We either do or we don't. We either train or we blow it off. We either go to class or we don't. We either study for the test or we don't. At the moment of choice our mind will play tricks on us. Our emotional right brain will offer convincing arguments like "you can get away with it just this one time." What an illusion. The heck with getting away with it! We crush that emotional nonsense by tuning into our levelheaded Big Dog, our competitor, and then make decisions that propel us forward, past being just average in life.

For those of us whose temperament is geared more toward work than play, we have an advantage. Personally, I love to practice. I truly enjoy working at getting better at something. For example, after retiring from many years of world-class weight lifting, I was looking for another sport to challenge my-

The Crossroads illustration (right) presents two paths in life: one that is dedicated to achieving and the other that is consumed with fun. Which path do you walk? Do you prepare and train or party and slug out? The choice is yours.

self with and found golf. I hit over one hundred balls every day, methodically worked my short game, and played several rounds a week until I achieved a legitimate three handicap. For me, that wasn't a grind. That was fun.

Additionally, those of us who are not overly social have a training advantage. For example, I'm not antisocial, but hanging out and partying has never been compelling to me, even as a teenager. So I've never had to seriously grapple with the work-or-socialize decision, to train or hang out. I've always naturally gravitated toward work. I see the decision of whether to go work or blow it off as being black or white. My inner voice says, "What's

The only way to recover and regenerate is through premium fueling and consistent, deep sleep.

your problem? Make the decision. Are you a champion or a slacker?"

My younger son Nick, who was eighteen at the time, was reading the first draft of this chapter and just shook his head and said, "Dad, you still don't get it, you're weird. Most of us don't think like you. For my friends and me, forgetting our

friends to go train is like solitary confinement. It's not a simple decision."

For many, this work-or-socialize battle is intense and fought with extreme anxiety, and frequently immediate fun interests are chosen over lifetime achievement interests. Many of your coaches, especially those who know how to win, will come across with a similar black-or-white mindset—either we do or we don't. The problem is many athletes get stuck in the middle, being pulled in both directions. Escaping Middleville is hard. It first requires a perspective that desires achievement, and then making disciplined decisions and getting to work.

Clarification: This book is not intended to help you feel better about your bad habits—its purpose is to give you the tools to become the competitor you have secretly wished you were. Hearing the stone-cold truth is how we progress.

So, how do we socialize less and train more? Here's the bottom line: As athletes, especially at the young adult level, we can't have it all. An athlete's commitments are triple those of most non-athletes. There just isn't enough time each day to get everything in, and getting consistent sleep is the main problem. Consistent, deep rest is crucial for athletes. We train, practice hard, lift weights, and condition. The only way to recover and regenerate is through premium fueling and consistent, deep sleep. Socializing and hanging out cut into sleep and can be devastating distractions. We have to get up at six or seven in the morning to go to school—or even earlier to work out before school—while our party friends are snug and warm, snoring in their beds. They have nothing to get up for except the next party. We're different.

Do you have the courage to be exceptional? Do you want/need to win so bad you get goose bumps? If we sincerely want to excel, if it truly is a burning desire in our gut we must make disciplined, balanced, black-or-white decisions that are *driven by your dream*.

Disciplined Balanced Decisions

Performing at a high level requires balance—that's the challenge. A balanced daily schedule requires conscious, focused, disciplined decisions and actions. There's no way around it.

Let's consider the definition of dis-ci-pline: an activity or exercise that develops or improves a skill. Genuinely disciplining ourselves is a rigorous, moment-by-moment task. What helps the process is being clear about what we're striving for and why nothing will get in our way of achieving it—*absolutely nothing*. Then it's much easier to say, "no thanks," to the constant barrage of social distractions and drag ourselves off the couch to get to work.

Does this mean we don't have a social life? Not at all! It's about balance. If you were talking to an Olympic or pro volleyball player you greatly respect and she was asking you about your dreams and goals for volleyball and how much practice and hard work you put in, what would you say? "Well, only enough that it doesn't get in the way of my social life"? How do you think she would respond? What do you think the look on her face would be?

 "There is no substitute for work, no short cuts to the top."
Frank Robinson

It's okay to hang with friends and blow off steam. But we must be deliberate and know what we're doing. We don't get lost in the party moment. We are not mindless fun seekers; we are high-stakes competitors seriously wanting to win. Competing at a high level takes a greater commitment than average folks are willing to put in. That commitment doesn't mean we become strangers to our friends and family. However, I've known and watched many great athletes fail because they were unable to give up socializing for training. I've also known and watched numerous successful athletes who were smart enough to figure out how to get in some hang time without disrupting their training schedule. In fact, I know of highly successful athletes who purposefully schedule in hang time to break up training and to give themselves a break. But they do it with purpose, not to avoid training.

Balance is the key, and when we have lots of entertainment options, ... disciplined decisions must be made.

Balance is the key, and when we have lots of entertainment options, which most of us do, disciplined decisions must be made. Our dream, supported by tangible goals, is what drives winning decisions.

Once you envision a real dream and decide with conviction that you can sacrifice daily social outings by separating yourself somewhat from the pleasure pack, I strongly recommend that you put together a daily/weekly schedule. Give yourself a framework to operate in. It can be as detailed as you like, which depends on your personality type. But give yourself a daily/weekly outline of what you *need* to do, along with what you *want* to do. Take a little time and do some planning. You'll be able to schedule in some hang time, just not as much as your party friends. That's why you'll be competitive and victorious. It truly is your decision. Set daily and weekly goals to achieve a significant dream, then diligently work at it

Dreams vs. Goals

Let's separate a dream from a goal. A dream is not a goal. Goals are short-term markers we use as targets on the way to accomplishing our dream. Our dream is more about what we're going to get from the goals and the

Daily Schedule	Champion	Slacker
6:15	Thirty-minute run	Sleep
7:15	Fuel	Still sleeping
7:50	School	Stll sleeping – skip school
12:30	Fuel	Junk food
1:10	Weight training	Smoke dope
2:50	Practice	Video games
5:30	Fuel	Junk food
6:00	Home work	Smoke more dope
7:00	Hang–out	Hang–out
9:45	MT Training	Hang–out
10:00	Lights out	Party time

CHAMPION VS. SLACKER

Take a little time and do some planning. You'll be able to schedule in some hang time, just not as much as your party friends. That's why you'll be competitive and victorious.

dedication, hard work, and personal sacrifice. Too often we only focus on goals, which tend to be bland and tasteless.

Our dream should be full of emotions, feelings, and glory. Our dream must be so big and real we can taste it. When we think about our dream, it should make our mouth water and the hair on the back of our neck stand up. Thinking about our dream should move the Grr Meter in the plus direction—it should be deeply motivating.

This is why many of us get lost. We don't create a vision of our future. It's very important to picture the future and to have a dream, so we have a counterargument against giving in to the short-term pursuit of fun, social indulgence, or laziness.

Consider this: Is the desire to be a champion a goal or a dream? It's a dream. A goal is striving for a double-double, to put up a personal best, make varsity, or practice setting, passing, and blocking one hour a day five days a week. All the things we'll get by accomplishing those goals and winning a title tournament are what drive our dream: ink in the local paper, maybe even some national press, a scholarship, or proving that when we put our mind to it, we can do something significant, like distinguishing ourselves as a champion. All those achievements set a tone for the rest of our life and the list of potential achievements is long. There are many examples of what one gets from achieving a big dream, but what's most important is for you to create *your* list of what *you'll* get from achieving your dream.

Example: Respond to these questions by filling in the blanks: "If I won..., I would get...," or "If I won..., I would be able to...," or "If I achieved..., then I would be the only person to...." Answering those questions in detail has a forward-looking perspective and produces mental pictures and feelings associated with potential achievement that are deeply motivating.

Dedicate yourself to achieving your dream. Make solid decisions that propel you toward success.

Here's another example. When you wanted your first car so bad it hurt, why was that desire so intense? Because you had tons of mental pictures and feelings of what it would be like to have a car: being free and independent, dating, and running around with your friends. Those feelings that went along with the thoughts of having a car were the core of your car dream. Then, you set a series of goals to get the car to live the dream.

Our dream drives our motivation, which leads to setting goals, which leads to working on our goals, which leads to achieving our dream. Make sense? A dream that we can taste, that we can believe we can achieve, is what motivates us to set goals and then to do the work to reach those goals. We find our motivation by creating a dream and knowing clearly what we want from accomplishing our dream.

So many of us struggle with doing what is necessary and giving it our all, every single day. Some days we're on and some days we're off. Some days we have a dream and its motivating force, but most days we don't. Okay, yeah, it's fun to socialize, but what do we gain from it other than relationship building and immediate gratification? Answer: absolutely nothing that will make us a better competitor or a champion. When we're feeling lazy and would rather blow off training and be a slug, what fires us up to take ourselves by the ear and get to work? Yep, a real dream, one that we must accomplish for our life to feel worthwhile.

THERE'S NOT ENOUGH TIME TO GET IT ALL IN.

HOURS

PUT WORK FIRST

Fun options are endless, and texting never stops. Put work first. There's just not enough time to get everything in. Make positive choices that propel you toward success.

Find your motivation. Why are you out for your sport? Why are you putting yourself through the long practices and social isolation? If it's just to do something or to hang with your athlete friends, that's okay, but that lacks the motivation to excel. Having a dream will drive you to make disciplined decisions to train more and play less. Without a dream, your core motivation, your fire, is dull and weak.

How powerful is your desire to achieve? How much heart do you have to push forward and train when your friends are giving up? Do you have the courage to strive for excellence? Ask yourself those questions and answer them truthfully. Then feel your commitment and dedication grow.

I hope this *dream to achieve* point is being expressed with maximum clarity. We need a dream to be able to say, "no thanks," to the social opportunities that present themselves every day and to overcome laziness so we can train and prepare. The clarity of our dream is what drives us to stay dedicated. If we don't have a real dream driving our desire to excel, and if the reasons why we want to achieve aren't *crystal clear*, then staying committed is a tremendous challenge—if we can stay committed at all. Our dream is our emotional power. A car dream is vivid and tangible. Our sports/future dream must have the same clarity and drawing power.

Here are some weak, non-dream examples for being out for volleyball:

1. It's something to do.

2. You have friends on the team.

3. Your mom or dad was an athlete.

4. Coach says, "You could be really good."

Here are some strong, big-dream examples:

1. You want to go to college and you need a scholarship.

2. You want to distinguish yourself as a person who can strive, persevere, and achieve.

3. You want to win a state or national tournament.

4. You want to be an elite athlete and make a living at what you love.

Once you think about it, even a little, there are many other examples of strong dreams. It's absolutely vital that you have a clear, vivid vision of your dream, and yes, every day it's a battle—turning down entertainment and lying-on-the-couch options requires disciplined decision-making.

Strong Dreams	Non-Dreams
• I want to go to college and need a scholarship	• It's something to do.
• I want to prove to myself and everyone else that I can be great at something.	• I have friends on the team.
• I want to distinguish myself as a person who can strive, perse-vere, and achieve.	• My mom or dad was an athlete.
• I want to be a pro athlete and make a living doing what I love.	• Coach says "You could be really good."

MOTIVATE YOURSELF

Without a strong dream driving our desire to excel, and if the reasons why aren't crystal clear, staying committed is a tremendous challenge—if we can stay committed at all. Dream big and motivate yourself!

Again, most people don't make courageous decisions that forsake immediate pleasure for long-term personal achievement.

Here's what you might be thinking: "I have a dream, but I still struggle with dedication and discipline." I know many of you feel that way. The missing ingredient is sacrifice

Sacrifice

If you do have a dream, want it really bad, and are motivated to get it, you might be thinking, "When I put this book down, I'm gonna go make things happen." But for those of you who are still being pulled in both directions, you must take hold of the *fact* that dedication and discipline require sacrificing. It's just the way it is.

Part of the quote from the football coach's email, "success is something achieved by the minority," really says it all. In order to be a champion at anything, we have to do things which elevate us above the average, things which require sacrifice. Sac-ri-fice: the surrender of something valued for the sake of something having a higher or more pressing claim.

DREAM big and commit. Your motivation depends on it, and your success demands it!

When we really want something bad, nothing gets in our way, right? We sacrifice certain things to get what we want. We don't accept "no" for an answer. We plot and plan and don't stop until we get what we want. We take action!

A simpler definition of sacrifice is that "less partying and more working equals achievement." Saying, "no thanks," to social invitations, or calling it a night long before others do is surrendering something valued—time with friends. No dream, no surrender. We must submit to the reality of striving for excellence. The bottom line is we can't have it all. It's just the way it is. And when we do commit and sacrifice, we will get everything in return—rewards most people only fantasize about having because they never take action or sacrifice to go get them. Most who resist committing and sacrificing usually don't accomplish much in life. Realize that committing to hard work and sacrificing hang time are key differences between becoming a champion or staying a contender. You, a champion, will submit yourself to the sacrifices of training, realizing that in order to acquire success—the results of a dream—sacrifices must be made.

Here's a no-sacrifice story. Several years ago I mentored a high school senior who was a gifted athlete, physically. He played a variety of sports from the time he could walk. Football and basketball ended up being his two primary interests. When he got to high school, he was heading down the party road and by his sophomore year was pretty much self-destructing. His junior year was a disaster. Academically he was a no-show, and of course he was not eligible for sports.

He had been a good friend of my son Nick since grammar school, and we ran into him the summer before his senior year. After he shared his personal story, we offered to take him in hoping that a fresh start and new environment would help him get back on track to finish high school and ultimately to go to college. At first, he was negative and reluctant. He thought he was too far behind—besides, there was no guarantee he would be eligible to play sports. I told him that to assume things in life is, well, ignorant, and suggested that with a couple of investigative phone calls he would know exactly what his options were. He agreed and within a couple of calls found out that he could enroll and was eligible. He moved in with us agreeing to my one condition—he had to go to school, no excuses. If he didn't, he'd have to move out.

He was pumped. He was back in school and on the football field again. Practice went great and he quickly earned a starting position at corner. He contributed in the first couple of games and was looking forward to a great season. Then the phone call came.

I thought I had kept in pretty close contact with him regarding attendance and what I heard was, "Are you kidding, I'm going to every class. Why would I blow this?" He'd lied. The athletic director told me he had been skipping class since the first day of school. His attendance record was barely 50%. Unfortunately, I had to ask him to move out. To keep up his end of the deal, all he had to do was go to class. There were no grade requirements. *Just go to class.*

Dedication, discipline, and sacrifice have to be your best friends if you want to succeed, at anything.

As I was discussing with him why he chose to skip school and blow the opportunity, he looked at me like I was some sort of idiot and said, "Because I want to have fun."

I'll never forget that—fun, at the expense of everything.

For whatever reason, it was more important for this young man to identify, connect with, and relate to kids who were consumed with socializing and partying than the kids who wanted to achieve and excel. At the time, he made undisciplined decisions and had to suffer the consequences.

"In reading the lives of great men ...self-discipline with all of them came first."

Harry S. Truman

If you're wondering why I didn't tell you an overcoming-the-obstacles, pump-you-up kind of story, it's because you hear those kinds of stories all of the time. It's like the Navy SEAL example; recruits don't get sent to inspiration school to learn how to overcome fear and intimidation, they get sent to learn-how-to-think school. Inspiring stories are cool, but they don't get at the reality of the issue, which is if you don't commit and sacrifice, you will not excel.

Over the course of the season, you'll be confronted many times with "do you?" or "don't you?" decisions.

• Point: dedication, discipline, and sacrifice have to be your best friends if you want to succeed—at anything.

Over the course of the season, you'll be confronted many times with "do you?" or "don't you?" decisions. Do you get up and go to school or sleep in? Do you follow through with scheduled mental toughness training or blow it off and hang out? Do you stay out late and party or go home and rest up for tomorrow's training? Each decision is a test, to slack off or get it done, to succumb to temptation or Grr up and fight back.

Your party friends will provide added pressure: "Come on, just hang out with us, you train all of the time." And of course you'll want to, which isn't a bad thing—you're human. But each time you let the temptation of partying and laziness cut into your training and preparation, you're jeopardizing your potential. Your irrational right brain will try to convince you that you've trained enough.

Muster the courage to quiet your right brain down by letting your Big Dog out. You're on a journey to become a unique member of our championship community—those who can overcome temptation and are willing to submit to the sacrifices required for higher achievements.

The Penn State University Hawkeyes volleyball team celebrate their victory over Stanford University Cardinals during the Division I Women's Volleyball Championship.
Photo by *Corbey R. Dorsey/NCAA Photos*

No doubt your decision record won't be perfect when the season is over. That's okay, perfection is not the goal. *Trying is the goal.* Make more positive decisions than negative. Make more decisions that propel you toward outstanding achievement than decisions that trap you among the average and mediocre.

Dream Big

Without a vivid picture of a real dream, it doesn't matter who tries to push you—you won't have the burning desire to make the difficult decisions that confront you every day.

Grasp the opportunity to better yourself by creating an achievable dream and then commit to the dedication, discipline, and sacrifice required to accomplish it.

Sam Huff said, "Discipline is the key to being successful. We all get twenty-four hours a day. It's up to us what we do with those twenty-four hours."

You've only got one life. Your future is yours and yours only, so dream big and commit—your motivation and emotional power depend on it, and your success demands it!

Now you know how to *dream* big—and achieve something extraordinary.

RISE ABOVE

7 DREAM

Don't be just "average." Commit to accomplishing outstanding achievements. Dream big!

TOURNAMENT PROCESS

Have your dream in the front of your mind.

FOCUS POINT

Make it happen. Follow your schedule.

THE BIG 3

SELF-TALK

"I've got to skip the party and go train."

VISUALIZE

Picture making decisions that lead to success.

ADAPT

Don't be a slacker. Sacrifice, work hard, and achieve.

WinningSTATE
The Mental Toughness Company

WinningSTATE Mental Toughness System
EXPECTATIONS

What to expect:

Now, you can prepare for the intensity of the competitive spotlight and the uneasiness of having all eyes focused on you. You can expect your *Winning-STATE* tournament process and specific focus points to give you a mentally tough skillset to handle the nerves. You can expect to use the adrenaline, the Superwoman juice to your advantage. You can expect to possess a mentally tough mental game to 100% believe in yourself, compete, and win.

What not to expect:

Similar to the first time you went to volleyball practice and didn't leave with a perfect kill shot, don't expect to completely conquer the nerves in one read. Be realistic. Don't expect huge leaps, expect small gains. Just like building physical skills, we must work at building mental toughness skills. Most importantly, don't expect solid results unless you take action and adapt.

Adapt:

Life, every day, is your practice arena; there are unlimited opportunities to practice and improve your "response" to nervy situations. First, be mentally active and get your head around the fundamentals of the *WinningSTATE* mental toughness system. Construct your tournament process and isolate your focus points. Be mentally active. Respond! Take charge of your mental state. Don't let unchecked emotional reactions get the best of you. Train your brain to respond to pressure-packed situations with poise and balance. Practice anticipating nervy situations, switching attitudes, narrowing your focus, replacing doubt with past success, and 100% believing in yourself. Clutch performances are in you. Compete mentally tough and believe!

WinningSTATE Mental Toughness Skills
QUICK REFERENCE

WinningSTATE
The Mental Toughness Company

SWITCH
GET FIERCE
Changes our attitude from friendly to confrontational
to fiercely compete and get the job done.

NARROW
ELIMINATE DISTRACTIONS
Blocks out distractions by focusing our mental
activities on SMS and our job at each battle zone.

FUEL
POWER YOUR PERFORMANCE
Makes fresh carbs and fats, and pure H_2O the priority
for quick decisions and fast recovery.

ANTICIPATE
LOVE THE NERVES
Exposes our primal competitive reaction, so we can
respond and use the adrenaline to our advantage.

REPLACE
DRAW ON SUCCESS
Shifts our focus from apprehension and doubt to our
past Big Dog success, so we can believe and execute.

BELIEVE
WIN THE BATTLE
Brings all of the skills together on game day
to handle the nerves, fiercely compete, and win.

DREAM
RISE ABOVE
Creates a life-changing dream to ignite our
motivation and drive our decisions.

winningstate.com

The WinningSTATE
MISSION

"To bring world-class mental toughness skills to every athlete in the world, to crush doubt, fiercely compete, and win."

From his first competition in 1977, *WinningSTATE* author Steve Knight was fascinated with the mental aspect of competing. Since he was not a physical phenom, he instinctively knew his mind is what would give him a competitive advantage. 35 years later this fascination with how to keep it together mentally when the pressure is high and the lights are white hot is what drives the *WinningSTATE* mission today: to bring world-class mental toughness skills to every athlete in the world, to crush doubt, fiercely compete, and win.

Our goal is to provide world-class mental toughness products that revolutionize how coaches and athletes prepare for nerve-racking competition.

We believe that performing at peak levels under pressure has more to do with mental toughness and less to do with confidence. In fact, confidence is overrated. And with this simple shift in thinking, from personal confidence to mental toughness skills, every athlete in the world can build a tournament process with specific focus points to bring order to a chaotic environment, believe in themselves, and execute.

Through *WinningSTATE mental toughness paper and audio books,* and the *WinningSTATE Online Mental Toughness Academy,* we are dedicated to creating and supplying ground-breaking mental toughness products athletes around the world use to crush doubt, fiercely compete, and win!

WinningSTATE is the world leader in mental toughness training for men's and women's sports.

The WinningSTATE MENTAL TOUGHNESS

SYSTEM

BE A MENTAL GAME GIANT

1 PERSPECTIVE
Winning is mental, not physical.

2 VOCABULARY
Words are a necessity, build mental toughness vocabulary.

3 TOURNAMENT PROCESS
Plan your job, start to finish.

4 FOCUS POINTS
Isolate what to think about.

5 SKILLS & ROUTINES
Know them like the backs of your hands.

6 CHECK IN
Use The Big 3 to stay in the present.

7 BELIEVE
We must do "it" ourselves.

MENTAL TOUGHNESS

Skills:	**Routines:**	**Objective:**
Switch, Narrow, Fuel, Anticipate, Replace, Believe, Dream	Competitive Breathing The SMS Sequence The 3 Battle Zones Adrenaline Routines	Crush doubt, fiercely compete, and win!

The Big 3: Self-talk, Visualize, Adapt.

Compete Mentally Tough!

WinningSTATE
The Mental Toughness Company

ANSWERS TO TOUGH QUESTIONS:

1 **What is a mental game?**

Making a clear distinction between our physical game and our mental game is vital. Our physical game centers on strength, speed, conditioning, agility, and physical skills. Our mental game is a different beast; our mental game centers on dealing with nerves and blocking out distractions.

Our mental game is what we use to boldly step into the competitive spotlight and say, "Watch this," and then actually do it. Our mental game includes the skills to overcome peoples' number one fear: performing in public. Like practice and competition, our physical game and our mental game do overlap, but they are as different as day and night. Practice is safe, competition is threatening. Practice is learn-time, competition is showtime. We must separate our physical game from our mental game.

There's no question that being competitive takes hard physical work: we must be strong, quick, well conditioned, and highly skilled. But being competitive also takes hard mental work: we must be fierce, focused, well fueled, responsive to the nerves, have our Big Dog success ready to shoot down any doubt, and be black belts in mental jujitsu to 100% believe in ourselves. We must be mental game giants with backbones of tempered steel able to withstand the paralyzing pressures of the competitive spotlight.

2 **Are mental toughness and confidence the same?**

No! Mental toughness and confidence are not the same. Confidence has very little to do with handling pressure. How we "feel" about ourselves (our confidence) will never offset all of the crazy stuff that goes on in our head as we face the glare of the public spotlight. We believe most athletes have some degree of confidence, but very few athletes possess the mental toughness to consistently get it done under the lights. Pressure-packed situations require mental toughness or apprehension and doubt crush our confidence and dominate our mental state, then we hesitate and come up short.

The enemy is not a lack of confidence; the enemy is lacking mental toughness and allowing apprehension to turn into doubt. Confidence is overrated. When we don't doubt, we're "confident." *WinningSTATE* athletes focus their mental weapons on crushing doubt, rather than trying to inflate their "confidence." Mental toughness and confidence are not the same.

3 How do we know if we're not mentally tough?

To answer that question we must first evaluate our typical reaction to performing in public. Do we fall victim to nerves, doubt, and distractions, or do we focus, believe, compete, and win? The difficulty is being truthful with ourselves, but once we do, we can get to work and improve.

Realize that everyone gets nervous, and that getting nervous does not mean we're mentally weak. Getting nervous is natural. When we want to do well and don't want to look bad, but are uncertain about the outcome, we get nervous. The mentally tough are those who face the nerves head on, then work the skills to better handle the heat. The mentally weak avoid evaluating their reactions to pressure, and rarely improve. The mentally tough don't fold under pressure.

Go to winningstate.com and watch the Navy SEAL video on the Watch page. Those SEAL recruits aren't acting like tough guys treating the potential of drowning like it's no big deal. They step up and tackle their primal super-fears head-on. They train their brain to deal with the extreme pressures of life or death situations. Actually doing it is being mentally tough.

WinningSTATE athletes work their mental game not because they're mentally weak or have some kind of confidence issue, but rather, because they're smart and giving themselves a competitive advantage—a mentally tough competitive advantage.

4 Do some have "it," and some don't?

The thinking that some have "it" and some don't, that only a select few are born with "the ability" to handle nerve-racking pressure is a myth. That thinking implies that our mental toughness, our fight-back power, is determined by our parents, who either pass along the mental toughness gene or they don't. Please. That thinking is missing the obvious: even world-class veterans, those who supposedly have "it," struggle with self-belief.

In a millisecond we all shift from believing to doubting and then back to believing and then back to doubting, emotionally flip flopping around like a fish out of water. Doubt in general is a constant issue for human beings, but especially for competitive athletes; our self-belief is on public display and it changes from moment to moment, month to month, and year to year.

We believe overcoming our "apprehensive" reactions, the primal first tendency for most of us, is the challenge. Most of us react negatively to any task that includes the potential of failure. Instead of focusing on what might go right, most of us dwell on what might go wrong. Most of us give in to thoughts and feelings of possible failure and embarrassment without any fight, and it's 100% in our heads. We all have "it." We need to attack your mental game like we attack our physical game to step up mentally tough, doubt free, and get the job done.

5 What is a tournament process?

A tournament process is an organized, systematic approach to competition. This is how we eliminate distractions and crush apprehension. Think about it. Practices are highly organized and very specific, but we go to tournaments (the reason we practice) without a clue of what to do. Our mental game is built around an organized tournament process that includes the evening before, the morning of, the stands/dugout, the on-deck circle and the batter's box. We use this tournament process along with specific focus points to narrow our concentration to what's important: *doubt-free execution*.

WinningSTATE athletes treat all competitive environments as hostile, high-distraction battlegrounds. We use our *WinningSTATE* tournament process to get our mind right. We mentally check in, switch attitudes, and focus our attention on getting ready for the next trip to the plate.

6 What are focus points?

Focus points are prepared mental targets we shift our thinking to when the nerves surge and the Doubt Demons swarm. Mental toughness under pressure, simply put, comes down to concentration. We're either consumed by distractions and apprehension or we're mentally tough, 100% focused on executing.

Professional golfer and on air analyst Paul Azinger put it well when he said, *"Concentration is not a gift. It doesn't come naturally. Concentration is a learned behavior. It's an art form. It's beautiful to watch."*

We agree. The elusive aspect of battlefield concentration is not "confidence," it's lacking "points" to concentrate on, which is the learned behavior part of Azinger's statement. Consider this: How can we expect ourselves to concentrate under pressure if we don't have anything to concentrate on? We can't. Our tournament process must include crunch-time mental routines that include specific focus points or the Doubt Demons have their way.

7 What is a *WinningSTATE* advantage?

A *WinningSTATE* advantage is having the ability to conquer the biggest problem in sports: the nerves. *WinningSTATE* athletes bring these mental toughness skills and routines to the battlefield: An organized tournament process. Specific focus points. A ritual to switch attitudes. Max energy. The SMS Sequence. Adrenaline Routines. Responsiveness to apprehension. The ability to draw on past success. All of which produce an unshakeable self-belief in their ability to compete, and win.

WinningSTATE athletes realize that they don't have to love the spotlight, but that they gotta love the nerves. They realize that pulling off clutch performances is an active, personal choice, not a random supernatural event. *WinningSTATE* athletes train themselves in the art of choosing to believe, rather than allowing themselves to doubt.

We believe that competing and winning is 90% mental, and that hard physical work is not the solution to handling nerve-racking pressure. We believe every athlete in the world has what it takes to pull off clutch performances, if they train themselves to be mentally tough when it's showtime.

WinningSTATE
The Mental Toughness Company

WinningSTATE Mental Toughness
VOCABULARY

7 WINNINGSTATE MENTAL TOUGHNESS SKILLS:

SWITCH: GET FIERCE

Changes our attitude from friendly to confrontational to fiercely compete and get the job done.

NARROW: ELIMINATE DISTRACTIONS

Blocks out distractions by focusing our mental activities on SMS and our job at each battle zone.

FUEL: POWER YOUR PERFORMANCE

Makes fresh carbs and fats, and pure H_2O the priority for quick decisions and fast recovery.

ANTICIPATE: LOVE THE NERVES

Exposes our primal competitive reaction, so we can respond and use the adrenaline to our advantage.

REPLACE: DRAW ON SUCCESS

Shifts our focus from apprehension and doubt to our past Big Dog success, so we can believe and execute.

BELIEVE: WIN THE BATTLE

Brings all of the skills together on tournament day to handle the nerves, fiercely compete, and win.

DREAM: RISE ABOVE

Creates a life-changing dream to ignite our motivation and drive our decisions.

TTOURNAMENT PROCESS: an organized, systematic approach to conquering the chaos and getting our mind right.

FOCUS POINTS: prepared mental activity we shift our thinking to, to block out distractions and conquer doubt.

THE BIG 3:

SELF-TALK: an internal conversation we use to influence our mental state—we give ourselves a pep talk.

VISUALIZE: we picture SMS and our Big Dog success to crush apprehension and pump up our self-belief.

ADAPT: we deliberately change the way we think about competing, and the way we respond to nerves.

MENTAL TOUGHNESS: the ability to confront doubts, fears, and adversity head on, and overcome them.

MENTAL JIU-JITSU: mentally tough grappling with the 3 Doubt Demons, and choking the dream-crushers out.

GO TIME: "a situation" when peak performance is needed.

ADRENALINE: a bodily hormone produced to elevate our "capabilities" during dangerous, high-stress encounters.

ATHLETE: someone who physically participates in sports.

COMPETITOR: someone who fiercely competes, not just physically participates in sports.

CLUTCH: a competitor's ability to deliver under pressure when it's all on the line.

DOUBT: a feeling of uncertainty or lack of conviction.

FIERCENESS: a strong, intense, unstoppable, confrontational attitude with deliberate execution.

PERFORMANCE: demonstrating a skill in front of an audience.

LEVELHEADED: rational, composed, and grounded under pressure.

MENTAL TOUGHNESS SKILL: a mental technique to deal with the high-stress pressure of competition.

NERVES: a primal adrenaline reaction to performing in public.

PRIMAL COMPETITIVE REACTION (PCR): to fight, flee, or freeze, our natural primal reactions to threatening encounters.

PHYSICAL TOUGHNESS: enduring the physical pain and exhaustion of training and competing.

GAME-TIME: when all eyes are on you, the opposite of practice.

PRESSURE: mental and emotional stress specific to competitive environments.

MELTDOWN: when pressure pushes a competitor's doubt and intimidation to the point of collapse.

POISE/COMPOSURE: the state of being mentally balanced and stable under pressure.

RIGHT BRAIN: our source of apprehension, doubt, and panicky emotional reactions under pressure.

LEFT BRAIN: the source of levelheaded, balanced, and poised responses under pressure.

COMPETITION: a contest between an individual or team to claim a trophy that cannot be shared.

COMPETITIVE: a confrontational, aggressive attitude that will battle to achieve.

PRACTICE: training and rehearsing sport and mental toughness skills.

3 DOUBT DEMONS:

> **EMBARRASSMENT:** fear of being laughed at.
>
> **INADEQUACY:** fear of not being good enough.
>
> **PAST FAILURE:** fear of repeating a poor performance.

BIG DOG: our doubt-free self, who pushes through apprehension, draws on success, welcomes the spotlight, focuses on the positive, believes, and executes.

BIG DOG DESCRIPTORS: daring, gutsy, brave, courageous, bold, assertive, decisive, deliberate, and mentally tough.

LITTLE DOG: our doubtful self, who succumbs to apprehension, worries about failure, dreads the spotlight, dwells on the negative, doesn't believe, and emotionally melts down.

LITTLE DOG DESCRIPTORS: timid, apprehensive, doubtful, hesitant, passive, afraid, cowardly, indecisive, and mentally weak.

BIG DOG VICTORY: when we overcome apprehension and doubt, and go for it.

FIGHT BACK: a mentally tough counterattack to combat apprehension and doubt.

3 BATTLE ZONES: a narrowing technique to block out distractions and focus on competing.

THE SMS SEQUENCE:

> **SITUATION:** our specific job at each battle zone.
>
> **MECHANICS:** our go-to fundamentals.
>
> **SUCCESS:** experiences when we overcame apprehension and doubt and went for it.

ADRENALINE ROUTINES: specific routines to help get our mind right before and during competition:

> **PLAN:** organize, list, and check off competition necessities as you pack.
>
> **FUEL:** make food choices that put energy first, flavor second.
>
> **REST:** purposefully getting horizontal for quick recovery.
>
> **BREATHE:** controlled, competitive breathing to calm nerves and focus thoughts.
>
> **REHEARSE:** visualize SMS and past Big Dog success.

FRESH FUEL: carbs and fats from unprocessed, natural sources to sustain max energy levels during competition.

CHAMPION: someone who is highly motivated, consistently works hard, and regards achievement as a necessity.

SLACKER: someone who is lazy, habitually avoids work, and regards achievement as a waste of time.

TOUGHEN UP: holding one's self accountable and not falling victim to apprehension and doubt.

COURAGE: the attitude that overcomes fear, pain, risk/danger, uncertainty, or intimidation.

PANSY: a mental weakling who lets apprehension and doubt dominate their reaction to confrontation.

GRR FACTOR: our raw internal power that drives our, "I can do this, nothing is stopping me" attitude.

DRAWING ON SUCCESS: deliberately remembering specific experiences of executing despite apprehension and doubt.

FUN CROWD: the individuals who are only motivated by fun, not personal achievement.

EVALUATING: examining inner/outer performance to improve and excel.

GETTING HORIZONTAL: resting flat on one's back to get maximum mental and physical recovery.

ATTITUDE: one's internal reaction to confrontation, either passive or assertive or something in between.

MS. CONGENIALITY: a typically pleasant, likable person who avoids confrontation.

BATTLE: a hostile meeting between opposing forces that requires a tenacious fight to take the prize.

TAKER: a competitive attitude that aggressively attacks the objective.

PROTECTOR: a competitive attitude that aggressively protects the objective.

POSTURING/ PROJECTING: a false bravado used to intimate an opponent that is typically an act, not an attitude.

CONFRONTATION: a hostile face-to-face encounter.

CONCENTRATION: laser-beam focus on a specific objective.

DISTRACTION: anything that obstructs focusing on a specific objective.

REACTION: unrestrained emotional outburst when confronted.

RESPONSE: taking thoughtful, deliberate action when confronted.

PREDICTABLE: behavior or events that occur in a way that is expected.

WinningSTATE
The Mental Toughness Company

Made in the USA
Middletown, DE
24 August 2024

59120270R00091